NEGRO MIGRATION
DURING THE WAR

Selected from
THE AMERICAN NEGRO: HIS HISTORY AND LITERATURE
William Loren Katz
GENERAL EDITOR

NEGRO MIGRATION DURING THE WAR

Emmett J. Scott

With a new preface by Thomas R. Cripps

ARNO PRESS and THE NEW YORK TIMES
NEW YORK 1969

EMMETT SCOTT'S "NEGRO MIGRATION DURING THE WAR" IS a remarkable book with pointed relevance to today's urban racial problems. First published in 1920, its whole format still has an amazing fidelity to the style and methods of recent studies. It represents an early effort of a private foundation, the Carnegie Endowment for Peace, to bring its resources to bear on a social problem. The foundation's work was given legitimacy and credibility by using the research skills of trained scholars from the black world, much as Gunnar Myrdal and later scholars focused on the problems of race by using trained Negro social scientists. Finally, the volume represents one of the first commitments of a university press (in this case, Oxford University Press) to the dissemination of data on social problems.

In the original Editor's Preface, David Kinley implies that the study benefited from an asset that many scholars now seem desirous to regain, the scientist's active involvement in the problems of his society. In the progressive era the faculties of urban universities, from Chicago to Columbia to Johns Hopkins, militantly announced their sympathy with the victims of the urban ghettos. As though in agreement, Kinley writes of Scott that he could best study the conditions of Negro migration because of "both his wide knowledge of the subject and his sympathy with the viewpoint of his race."

Scott presented an excellent and enduring monograph, partly because he brought to the project both organizational skills and writing experience. He had been editor of *The Texas Freeman*; a secretary, assistant, and ghost writer for Booker T. Washington; a faithful campaigner and publicist for the Republican National Committee; a member of the United States Liberian

Commission of 1909; caretaker executive at Tuskegee after Washington's death; and, at the time of his study, was Secretary-Treasurer of Howard University. Also, he employed the services and resources of such good men as Monroe W. Work, Director of the Division of Records and Research at Tuskegee Institute; Charles S. Johnson, then a young Negro graduate student at the University of Chicago; Timothy Thomas Fortune, a writer and former editor of *The New York Age* and advisor and friend of Booker T. Washington; Robert E. Park, the sociologist, who was President of the Chicago Urban League.

Scott completed his work at a time of deep crisis for American cities. For the modern reader many of the same conditions may still exist, but even though studies continue to flow from scholars' typewriters, Scott's work is still a sound primer. His team and he were among the first to observe racial problems on a national urban basis. They applied interdisciplinary concepts to their milieu that are still impressive. They brought together in convenient form the data from numerous cities. They carefully noted feedback effects on the rural South from which many Negroes had migrated. And last, they gathered a useful bibliography of the best monographs on the various cities to which Negroes were moving, pamphlets issued by the many public and private social welfare agencies, periodical literature, and a generous sampling of newspaper materials.

Negro Migration During the War is not without the flaws one expects from so old a work, but they are minor and even useful for pointing out important still unanswered questions. For example, modern measures of quantitative change, such as Shevsky-Bell topologies, were unavailable. Scott developed no clear concept of public opinion, which here is excerpted rather than systematically sampled. The researchers seem not to have studied migration into southern cities except as they served as way stations on the way to Chicago or Detroit. And finally there is the blind accident of the completion of the study too soon to consider the impact of the rash of riots that scarred American cities in the "red summer" of 1919; the reader is shown conditions in Chicago, however, with a sense of impending doom.

But no understandable and fortuitous omissions should stand in the way of the scholar and the general reader who may still read Scott with profit. This is especially true when one realizes that so much that Scott reported was confirmed in the next decade by the work of the University of Chicago urban sociologists (*The Negro in Chicago*), United States census abstracts on the Negro, and the local studies that followed in the wake of the 1919 riots.

Thomas R. Cripps
PROFESSOR OF HISTORY
MORGAN STATE UNIVERSITY

FOREWORD

In the preparation of this study I have had the encouragement and support of Dr. Robert R. Moton, Principal of the Tuskegee Normal and Industrial Institute, Alabama, who generously placed at my disposal the facilities of the Institute's Division of Records and Research, directed by Mr. Monroe N. Work, the editor of the *Negro Year Book*. Mr. Work has cooperated with me in the most thoroughgoing manner. I have also had the support of the National League on Urban Conditions and particularly of the Chicago branch of which Dr. Robert E. Park is President and of which Mr. T. Arnold Hill is Secretary. Mr. Hill placed at my disposal his first assistant, Mr. Charles S. Johnson, graduate student of the University of Chicago, to whom I am greatly indebted. I must also make acknowledgment of my indebtedness to Dr. Carter G. Woodson, Director of the Association for the Study of Negro Life and History, Incorporated, Washington, D. C., for placing at my disposal the facilities of his organization.

The work of investigation was divided up by assigning Mr. Work to Alabama, Georgia and Florida; Mr. Johnson to Mississippi and to centers in Missouri, Illinois, Wisconsin and Indiana, while the eastern centers were assigned to Mr. T. Thomas Fortune, Trenton, New Jersey, a former editor of the *New York Age,* and a publicist and investigator of well known ability. It is upon the reports submitted by these investigators that this study rests. I can not speak too warmly of the enthusiastic and painstaking care with which these men have labored to secure the essential facts with regard to the migration of the negro people from the South.

EMMETT J. SCOTT.

WASHINGTON, D. C.,
June 5, 1919.

vii

CONTENTS

NEGRO MIGRATION DURING THE WAR

CHAPTER I

Introduction

Within the brief period of three years following the outbreak of the great war in Europe, more than four hundred thousand negroes suddenly moved north. In extent this movement is without parallel in American history, for it swept on thousands of the blacks from remote regions of the South, depopulated entire communities, drew upon the negro inhabitants of practically every city of the South, and spread from Florida to the western limits of Texas. In character it was not without precedent. In fact, it bears such a significant resemblance to the migration to Kansas in 1879 and the one to Arkansas and Texas in 1888 and 1889 that this of 1916-1917 may be regarded as the same movement with intervals of a number of years.

Strange as it might seem the migration of 1879 first attracted general notice when the accusation was brought that it was a political scheme to transplant thousands of negro voters from their disfranchisement in the South to States where their votes might swell the Republican majority. Just here may be found a striking analogy to one of the current charges brought against the movement nearly forty years later. The congressional inquiry which is responsible for the discovery of the fundamental causes of the movement was occasioned by this charge and succeeded in proving its baselessness.[1]

The real causes of the migration of 1879 were not far to seek. The economic cause was the agricultural depression in the lower Mississippi Valley. But by far the most potent factor in effecting the movement was the treatment received by negroes at the hands of the South. More specifically, as expressed by the leaders of the movement and refugees themselves, they were a long series of oppression, injustice and violence extending over

[1] *Congressional Record,* 46th Cong., 2d sess., vol. X, p. 104.

3

a period of fifteen years; the convict system by which the courts are permitted to inflict heavy fines for trivial offenses and the sheriff to hire the convicts to planters on the basis of peonage; denial of political rights; long continued persecution for political reasons; a system of cheating by landlords and storekeepers which rendered it impossible for tenants to make a living, and the inadequacy of school facilities.[1] Sworn public documents show that nearly 3,500 persons, most of whom were negroes, were killed between 1866 and 1879, and their murderers were never brought to trial or even arrested. Several massacres of negroes occurred in the parishes of Louisiana. Henry Adams, traveling throughout the State and taking note of crime committed against negroes, said that 683 colored men were whipped, maimed or murdered within eleven years.[2]

In the year 1879, therefore, thousands of negroes from Mississippi, Louisiana, Texas, Alabama, Tennessee and North Carolina moved to Kansas. Henry Adams of Shreveport, Louisiana, an uneducated negro but a man of extraordinary talent, organized that year a colonization council. He had been a soldier in the United States Army until 1869 when he returned to his home in Louisiana and found the condition of negroes intolerable. Together with a number of other negroes he first formed a committee which in his own words was intended to " look into affairs and see the true condition of our race, to see whether it was possible we could stay under a people who held us in bondage or not." This committee grew to the enormous size of five hundred members. One hundred and fifty of these members were scattered throughout the South to live and work among the negroes and report their observations. These agents quickly reached the conclusion that the treatment the negroes received was generally unbearable.[3] Some of the conditions reported were that land rent was still high; that in the part of the country where the committee was organized the people were still being whipped, some of them by their former owners; that they were cheated out of their crops and that in

[1] *Atlantic Monthly*, LXIV, p. 222; *Nation*, XXVIII, pp. 242, 386.
[2] Williams, *History of the Negro Race*, II, p. 375.
[3] *Atlantic Monthly*, LXIV, p. 222.

some parts of the country where they voted they were being shot.

It was decided about 1877 that all hope and confidence that conditions could be changed should be abandoned. Members of this committee felt that they could no longer remain in the South, and decided to leave even if they "had to run away and go into the woods." Membership in the council was solicited with the result that by 1878 there were ninety-eight thousand persons from Louisiana, Mississippi, Alabama and Texas belonging to the colonization council and ready to move.[1]

About the same time there was another conspicuous figure working in Tennessee—Benjamin or "Pap" Singleton, who styled himself the father of the exodus. He began the work of inducing negroes to move to the State of Kansas about 1869, founded two colonies and carried a total of 7,432 blacks from Tennessee. During this time he paid from his own pocket over $600 for circulars which he distributed throughout the southern States. "The advantages of living in a free State" were the inducements offered.[2]

The movement spread as far east as North Carolina. There a similar movement was started in 1872 when there were distributed a number of circulars from Nebraska telling of the United States government and railroad lands which could be cheaply obtained. This brief excitement subsided, but was revived again by reports of thousands of negroes leaving the other States of the South for Kansas. Several hundred of these migrants from North Carolina were persuaded en route to change their course and go to Indiana.[3]

Much excitement characterized the movement. One description of this exodus says:

Homeless, penniless and in rags, these poor people were thronging the wharves of St. Louis, crowding the steamers on the Mississippi River, hailing the passing steamers and imploring them for a passage to the land of freedom, where the rights of citizens are respected and honest toil rewarded by honest compensation. The newspapers were filled with accounts of their

[1] Williams, *History of the Negro Race,* II, p. 375.
[2] W. L. Fleming, "Pap Singleton, the Moses of the Colored Exodus," *American Journal of Sociology,* chapter XV, pp. 61-82.
[3] *Congressional Record,* Senate Reports, 693, part II, 46th Cong., 2d sess.

destitution, and the very air was burdened with the cry of distress from a class of American citizens flying from persecution which they could no longer endure. Their piteous tales of outrage, suffering and wrong touched the hearts of the more fortunate members of their race in the North and West, and aid societies, designed to afford temporary relief and composed almost wholly of colored people, were organized in Washington, St. Louis, Topeka and various other places.[1]

Men still living, who participated in this movement, tell of the long straggling procession of migrants, stretching to the length at times of from three to five miles, crossing States on foot. Churches were opened all along the route to receive them. Songs were composed, some of which still linger in the memory of survivors. The hardships under which they made this journey are pathetic. Yet it is estimated that nearly 25,000 negroes left their homes for Kansas.[2]

The exodus during the World War, like both of these, was fundamentally economic, though its roots were entangled in the entire social system of the South. It was hailed as the " Exodus to the Promised Land " and characterized by the same frenzy and excitement. Unlike the Kansas movement, it had no conspicuous leaders of the type of the renowned " Pap " Singleton and Henry Adams. Apparently they were not needed. The great horde of restless migrants swung loose from their acknowledged leaders. The very pervasiveness of the impulse to move at the first definite call of the North was sufficient to stir up and carry away thousands before the excitement subsided.

Despite the apparent suddenness of this movement, all evidence indicates that it is but the accentuation of a process which has been going on for more than fifty years. So silently indeed has this shifting of the negro population taken place that it has quite escaped popular attention. Following the decennial revelation of the census there is a momentary outburst of dismay and apprehension at the manifest trend in the interstate migration of negroes. Inquiries into the living standards of selected groups of negroes in large cities antedating the migration of 1916-1917 have revealed from year to year an in-

---

[1] *American Journal of Social Science*, XI, pp. 22-35.
[2] *Ibid.*, p. 23.

creasing number of persons of southern birth whose length of residence has been surprisingly short. The rapid increase in the negro population of the cities of the North bears eloquent testimony to this tendency. The total increase in the negro population between 1900 and 1910 was 11.2 per cent. In the past fifty years the northern movement has transferred about 4 per cent of the entire negro population; and the movement has taken place in spite of the negro's economic handicap in the North. Within the same period Chicago increased her negro population 46.3 per cent and Columbus, Ohio, 55.3 per cent. This increase was wholly at the expense of the South, for the rural communities of the North are very sparsely populated with negroes and the increment accruing from surplus birth over deaths is almost negligible.[1]

When any attempt is made to estimate the volume of this most recent movement, however, there is introduced a confusing element, for it can not definitely be separated from a process which has been in operation since emancipation. Another difficulty in obtaining reliable estimates is the distribution of the colored population over the rural districts. It is next to impossible to estimate the numbers leaving the South even on the basis of the numbers leaving the cities. The cities are merely concentration points and they are continually recruiting from the surrounding rural districts. It might be stated that 2,000 negroes left a certain city. As a matter of fact, scarcely half that number were residents of the city. The others had moved in because it was easier to leave for the North from a large city, and there was a greater likelihood of securing free transportation or traveling with a party of friends. It is conservatively stated, for example, that Birmingham, Alabama, lost 38,-000 negroes. Yet within a period of three months the negro population had assumed its usual proportions again.[2]

Prior to the present migration of negroes, there was somewhat greater mobility on the part of the white than on the part of the negro population. As for example, according to

---

[1] *The Censuses of the United States.*
[2] *Ibid.*

the census of 1910 of 68,070,294 native whites, 10,366,735 or 15.2 per cent were living in some other division than that in which they were born. Of 9,746,043 native negroes reported by the census of 1910. 963,153 or 9.9 per cent were living outside the division of birth.[1] Previous to the present migration, the south Atlantic and the east south central divisions were the only ones which had suffered a direct loss in population through the migration of negroes.[2]

The census of 1910 brought out the fact that there had been considerable migration from the North to the South, as well as from the South to the North, and from the East to the West. The number of persons born in the North and living in the South (1,449,229) was not very different from the number born in the South and living in the North (1,527,107). The North, however, has contributed more than five times as many to the population of the West as the South has. The number of negroes born in the South and living in the North in 1910 was 415,533, or a little over two-thirds of the total number living in the North. Of the 9,109,153 negroes born in the South, 440,534, or 4.8 per cent, were, in 1910, living outside the South.[3] The migration southward it will be noted, has been in recent years largely into the west south central division, while the migration northward has been more evenly distributed by divisions, except that a comparatively small number from the South have gone into the New England States.[4]

The greater mobility of whites than of negroes is shown by the fact that in 1910, 15 per cent of the whites and 10 per cent of the negroes lived outside of the States in which they were born. This greater mobility of the whites as compared with the negroes was due in a large measure to the lack of opportunities for large numbers of negroes to find employment in the sections outside the South. The World War changed these conditions and gave to the negroes of the United States the same opportunities for occupations in practically every section

[1] Vol. I, census of 1910, Population, General Report and Analysis, p. 693.
[2] Ibid., p. 694.
[3] Ibid., p. 698.
[4] Vol. I, 1910 census, Population, General Report and Analysis, p. 699.

of the country, which had heretofore been enjoyed only by the whites. In 1900, 27,000 negroes born in the North lived in the South. In 1910, 41,000 negroes born in the North lived in the South. This indicated that there was beginning to be a considerable movement of negroes from the North to the South because of the greater opportunities in the South to find employment in teaching, medicine and business. The migration conditions brought about by the war have probably changed this to some extent. Previous to the World War, the States having the greatest gain from negro migration were Arkansas, 105,500, Pennsylvania, 85,000, Oklahoma, 85,000, Florida, 84,000, New York, 58,450 and Illinois, 57,500.

The point brought out here indicates that because of economic opportunities, Arkansas and Oklahoma, being contiguously situated in one section of the South and Florida in another section of the South, had received a greater migration of negroes than any State in the North.

Dr. William Oscar Scroggs of Louisiana calls attention to the tendency of negroes to move within the South, although, as he points out, this tendency is not as great as it is for the whites. On this he says:

The negro shows a tendency, not only to move northward, but also to move about very freely within the South. In fact, the region registering the largest net gain of negroes in 1910 from this interstate movement was the west south central division (Arkansas, Louisiana, Oklahoma and Texas) which showed a gain from this source of 194,658. The middle Atlantic division came second with a gain of 186,384, and the east north central third with a gain of 119,649. On the other hand, the south Atlantic States showed a loss of 392,827, and the east south central States a loss of 200,876 from interstate migration. While the negroes have shown this marked inclination toward interstate movement, they nevertheless exhibit this tendency in less degree than do the whites.[1]

The subjoined tables show the intersectional migration of the negro population:

[1] Scroggs, "Interstate Migration of Negro Population," *Journal of Political Economy*, December, 1917, p. 1040.

INTERSECTIONAL MIGRATION OF NEGROES

(As Reported by Census of 1910)

NUMBER BORN IN SPECIFIED DIVISIONS AND LIVING IN OR OUT OF THESE DIVISIONS

Division	Total Born in the Division	Number Living:		Per Cent Living Without the Division in Which Born
		Within Division	Without Division	
United States	9,746,043	8,782,890	963,153	9.9
New England	37,799	30,815	6,984	18.5
Middle Atlantic ...	212,145	189,962	22,183	10.5
East North Central	173,226	145,187	28,039	16.2
West North Central	198,116	162,054	36,062	18.2
South Atlantic	4,487,313	4,039,173	448,140	10.0
East South Central	2,844,598	2,491,607	352,991	12.4
West South Central	1,777,242	1,713,888	63,354	3.6
Mountain	7,342	4,122	3,220	43.9
Pacific	8,262	6,082	2,180	26.4

NUMBER LIVING IN SPECIFIED DIVISIONS

Division	Total Living in the Division	Number Born in and Living in the Division	Number Living in the Division Born in Other Divisions	Per Cent Living in Division Born in Other Divisions
United States	9,746,043	8,782,890	963,153	9.9
New England	58,109	30,815	27,294	47.0
Middle Atlantic ...	398,529	189,962	208,567	52.3
East North Central	292,875	145,187	147,688	50.4
West North Central	238,613	162,054	76,559	32.1
South Atlantic	4,094,486	4,039,173	55,313	1.4
East South Central	2,643,722	2,491,607	152,115	5.8
West South Central	1,971,900	1,713,888	258,012	13.1
Mountain	20,571	4,122	16,449	80.0
Pacific	27,238	6,082	21,156	77.7

MIGRATION NORTH TO SOUTH, SOUTH TO NORTH AND EAST TO WEST

Race and Section of Residence	Total Native Population	Born in:			State of Birth not Reported or Born in Outlying Possessions, etc.
		The North	The South	The West	
All Races					
United States	78,456,380	46,179,002	29,010,255	2,906,162	360,961
The North	44,390,371	42,526,162	1,527,107	124,001	213,101
The South	28,649,319	1,449,229	27,079,282	38,230	82,578
The West	5,416,690	2,203,611	403,866	2,743,931	65,282
White					
United States	68,386,412	45,488,942	19,814,860	2,766,492	316,118
The North	43,319,193	41,891,353	1,110,245	116,939	200,656
The South	19,821,249	1,407,262	18,326,236	34,523	53,228
The West	5,245,970	2,190,327	378,379	2,615,030	62,234
Negro					
United States	9,787,424	621,286	9,109,153	15.604	41,381
The North	999,451	570,298	415,533	2,295	11,325
The South	8,738,858	39,077	8,668,619	2,412	28,750
The West	49,115	11,911	25,001	10,897	1,306

NET MIGRATION EASTWARD AND WESTWARD AND
NORTHWARD AND SOUTHWARD

Section	Population, 1910					
	Total	White			Negro	All Other
		Total	Of Native Parentage	Of Foreign or Mixed Parentage		
Born east and living west of the Mississippi River ...	5,276,879	4,941,529	3,846,940	1,094,589	331,031	4,319
Born west and living east of the Mississippi River ...	684,773	616,939	417,541	199,398	63,671	4,163
Net migration westward across the Mississippi River	4,592,106	4,324,590	3,429,399	895,191	267,360	156
Born North and living South	1,449,229	1,407,262	1,156,122	251,140	39.077	2,890
Born South and living North	1,527,107	1,110.245	944,572	165,673	415.533	1,329
Net migration southward	....	297,017	211,550	85,467	....	1,561
Net migration northward	77,878	....	....	....	376,456	....

CHAPTER II

Causes of the Migration

It seems particularly desirable in any study of the causes of the movement to get beneath the usual phraseology on the subject and find, if possible, the basis of the dissatisfaction, and the social, political and economic forces supporting it. It seems that most of the causes alleged were present in every section of the South, but frequently in a different order of importance. The testimony of the migrants themselves or of the leading white and colored men of the South was in general agreement. The chief points of disagreement were as to which causes were fundamental. The frequency with which the same causes were given by different groups is an evidence of their reality.

A most striking feature of the northern migration was its individualism. This factor after all, however, was economic. The motives prompting the thousands of negroes were not always the same, not even in the case of close neighbors. As a means of making intelligible these complicating factors it is necessary to watch the process as it affected the several migrants. The economic motive stands among the foremost reasons for the decision of the group to leave the South. There are several ways of arriving at a conclusion regarding the economic forces. These factors might, for example, be determined by the amount of unemployment or the extent of poverty in a community as registered by the prosperity. These facts are important, but may or may not account wholly for individual action. Except in a few localities of the South there was no actual misery and starvation. Nor is it evident that those who left would have perished from want had they remained. Discontent became more manifest as comparisons were made between the existing state of things at home and a much better state of things elsewhere. It is possible to note in the appeals of the letters a suggestion of a desire simply to improve their living standards so long as there was an opportunity. In the case of some there is expressed a praiseworthy providence for their families; and in others may be found an index to the poverty and hopelessness of their home communities. In this type of migration the old order is strangely reversed. Large numbers of negroes have frequently moved around from State to State and even within the States of the South in search of more remunerative employment. A movement to the West or even about in the South could have proceeded from the same cause, as in the case of the migration to Arkansas and Oklahoma.

Among the immediate economic causes of the migration were the labor depression in the South in 1914 and 1915 and the large decrease in foreign immigration resulting from the World War. Then came the cotton boll weevil in the summers of 1915 and 1916, greatly damaging the cotton crop over considerable area, largely in Louisiana, Mississippi, Alabama, Georgia and Florida, and threatening greatly to unsettle farming conditions in the year 1917.[1] There followed then the cotton price demoralization and the low price of this product during subsequent years. The unusual floods during the summer of 1915 over large sections in practically the same States further aggravated the situation. The negroes, moreover, were generally dissatisfied because of the continued low wages which obtained in the South in spite of the increasing cost of living. Finally, there was a decided decrease in foreign immigration. The result was a great demand in the North for the labor of the negro at wages such as he had never received.[2]

To understand further the situation in the South at the beginning of the migration and just prior to it, attention should be directed to the fact that the practice of mortgaging the cotton crop before it is produced made sudden reversals—an inevitable result of such misfortune as followed the boll weevil and the floods. Thousands of landlords were forced to dismiss their tenants and close the commissaries from which came the

[1] *New York Times*, September 5, 9, 28, 1916.
[2] *Ibid.*, October 18, 28; November 5, 7, 12, 15; December 4, 9, 1916.

daily rations. Some planters in Alabama and Mississippi advised their tenants to leave and even assisted them. The banks and merchants refused to extend credit when cotton was no longer to be had as a security. As a consequence, a great number of tenants were left without productive work, money or credit. A host of idle persons thrown suddenly on the labor market could have no other effect than to create an excess in the cities to which they flocked, make laborers easily replaceable, and consequently reduce wages. A southern paper in commenting on this situation declared " there is nothing for this excess population to do. These people must live on the workers, making the workers poorer . . . if there is a tap that will draw off the idle population, that will be a good thing for the cities at least." [1]

The circumstances of unemployment which contributed so largely to the restless mood in some sections of the South was due primarily to a lack of sufficient capital to support labor during the lean seasons. This meant, of course, that the cotton pests and storms that played havoc with whole sections rendered helpless all classes of the population. The usual method of handling labor, especially on the cotton plantations, was for the planter to maintain his hands from the commissary during the fall and early winter in order that they might be convenient for the starting and cultivation of a new crop. But with their last year's crop lost, their credit gone and the prospects of a new crop very shadowy, there was left no other course but to dismiss the people whom they could not support.

For a long time southern farmers had been importuned to adopt a more diversified method of farming to offset the effects of unexpected misfortune in the cotton industry and to preserve the value of the soil. Following the ravages of the boll weevil, the idea gained wide application. The cotton acreage was cut down and other crops substituted. The cultivation of cotton requires about five times as many laborers as the cultivation of corn and the work is fairly continuous for a few employes throughout the year. Additional unemployment for negro ten-

[1] Work, *Report on Negro Migration from Alabama.*

ant farmers was an expected result of this diversification. The greatest immediate disadvantage to negro planters and small farmers resulting from the failure of the cotton crops was the lack of money and credit to sustain them while the corn and velvet beans were being grown. It was for like reasons impracticable to attempt to raise stock, for there was no means of making a beginning, as a certain amount of capital was prerequisite.

Despite the fact that food prices began to rise with the war, wages advanced very slowly. In 1915, wages of farm laborers in the South averaged around 75 cents a day. In the towns the principal opportunities for employment were in the oil mills, lumber mills, cotton compresses, railroad shops and domestic service. In the mills and shops the average of wages ranged from $1 to $1.50 a day. The wages of such skilled laborers as carpenters and bricklayers ranged from $2 to $3.50 a day. In domestic service women received from $1.50 to $3 per week and board. Men in domestic service received on an average of $5 a week.[1]

In spite of these conditions in the South it might appear strange that not until fifty years after the privilege was granted negroes to go where they pleased did they begin to make a sudden rush for the northern States. Stranger still does it seem that, despite the fairly general agreement among southern negroes that the North affords greater personal liberty, is less prejudiced to individuals because of the color of their skins, grants to negroes something nearer to open handed justice, participation in the government, wider privileges and freer associations, there should be in 1910 scarcely more than one-tenth of the negro population where these reputed advantages are. The North has been looked upon as the "Promised Land," the "Ark of Safety," the "House of Refuge" for all these years. A common reason recently advanced by the majority of southern negroes for the abandonment of their homes was the desire to escape from the oppressive social system of their section. Why have they not escaped before? The answer lies in the very hard

[1] Work and Johnson, *Report on the Migration during the World War.*

fact that, though the North afforded larger privileges, it would not support negroes. It was the operation of an inexorable economic law, confused with a multitude of social factors, that pushed them back to the soil of the South despite their manifest desire to leave it.

None of the causes was more effective than that of the opportunity to earn a better living. Wages offered in the North were double and treble those received in the South. Women who received $2.50 a week in domestic service could earn from $2.10 to $2.50 a day and men receiving $1.10 and $1.25 a day could earn from $2.50 to $3.75 a day in the various industries in the North.[1] An intensive study of the migration to Pitts-

[1] Attractive advertisements appeared in negro newspapers with wide circulation in the South. These are from the *Chicago Defender*.

"Wanted—10 molders. Must be experienced. $4.50 to $5.50 per day. Write B. F. R. *Defender* Office."

"Wanted—25 girls for dishwashing. Salary $7 a week and board. John R. Thompson, Restaurant, 314 South State Street. Call between 7 and 8 a.m. Ask for Mr. Brown."

"Wanted—25 young men as bus boys and porters. Salary $8 per week and board. John R. Thompson, Restaurant, 314 South State Street. Call between 7 and 8 a.m. Ask for Mr. Brown."

"Molders wanted. Good pay, good working conditions. Firms supply cottages for married men. Apply T. L. Jefferson, 3439 State Street.

"Ten families and 50 men wanted at once for permanent work in the Connecticut tobacco fields. Good wages. Inquire National League on Urban Conditions among Negroes, 2303 Seventh Avenue, New York City, New York."

"Molders wanted. A large manufacturing concern, ninety miles from Chicago, is in need of experienced molders. Wages from $3 to $5.50. Extra for overtime. Transportation from Chicago only. Apply Chicago League on Urban Conditions among Negroes. T. Arnold Hill, Executive Secretary, 3719 State Street, Chicago."

"Laborers wanted for foundry, warehouse and yard work. Excellent opportunity to learn trades, paying good money. Start $2.50—$2.75 per day. Extra for overtime. Transportation advanced from Chicago only. Apply Chicago League on Urban Conditions among Negroes, 3719 South State Street. Chicago?"

"Experienced machinists, foundrymen, pattern makers wanted, for permanent work in Massachusetts. Apply National League on Urban Conditions among Negroes, 2303 7th Ave., New York City."

"3,000 laborers to work on railroad. Factory hires all race help. More positions open than men for them."

"Men wanted at once. Good steady employment for colored. Thirty and 39½ cents per hour. Weekly payments. Good warm sanitary quarters free. Best commissary privileges. Towns of Newark and Jersey City. Fifteen minutes by car line offer cheap and suitable homes for men with families. For out of town parties of ten or more cheap transportation will be arranged. Only reliable men who stay on their job are wanted. Apply

burgh, made by Mr. Abraham Epstein, gives an idea of the difference in wages paid in the North and the South. His findings may be quoted: " The great mass of workers get higher wages here than in the places from which they come. Fifty-six per cent received less than two dollars a day in the South, while only five per cent received such wages in Pittsburgh." Sixty-two per cent received between $2 and $3 per day in Pittsburgh as compared with 25 per cent in the South, and 28 per cent received between $3 and $3.60 in this city as compared with four per cent in the South.

The inability to educate their children properly because of the inadequacy of school facilities was another cause which has been universally given for leaving the South.[1] The basis for this frequently voiced complaint is well set forth in the study of *Negro Education* by Dr. Thomas Jesse Jones.[2]

or write Butterworth Judson Corporation, Box 273, Newark, New Jersey, or Daniel T. Brantley, 315 West 119th Street, New York City."

" $3.60 per day can be made in a steel foundry in Minnesota, by strong, healthy, steady men. Open only to men living in Chicago. Apply in person. Chicago League on Urban Conditions among Negroes, 3719 South State Street, Chicago, Illinois."

[1] An investigator in Mississippi reports the following:

The school population is 60 per cent colored. There are seven white and two colored schools. The average salaries paid to white assistant teachers is $75 per month. The average salaries paid to colored assistant teachers is $32.50 per month. The average number of pupils taught by white is 30 and the average number taught by colored is 100.

In the county there are no agricultural high schools or in fact high schools of any kind. The whites in the same county have an agricultural high school of "magnificent proportions" and "excellent facilities," a literary high school and about ten consolidated schools.

Negroes complain that the authorities are building white schools in communities where the negro population is five times as great. When they first sought to establish these consolidated schools, there was a provision that every one must pay taxes to support them. Negroes who were required to pay large taxes refused because they were denied the benefits of the schools. A law was passed with the provision that the majority of qualified electors in a county supervisor's district might secure one of these schools on petition to the Board of Supervisors and with the understanding that they would pay taxes. But negroes are not qualified electors and consequently have no schools.

In Liberty Grove the white school goes to the twelfth grade, with courses also in music. Automobiles bring the children to school and carry them back. The negro school in the same community has only one teacher getting $25 per month and teaching over 200 children. There are two large negro denominational schools, Jackson College and Campbell College which serve to supplement the public schools provided by the city.

[2] Jones, *Negro Education*, vol. II, pp. 14, 15, Bulletin, 1916, No. 30 of the United States Bureau of Education.

The inadequacy of the elementary school system for colored children is indicated both by the comparisons of public appropriations already given and by the fact that the attendance in both public and private schools is only 58.1 per cent of the children six to fourteen years of age. The average length of the public school term is less than five months in practically all of the southern States. Most of the school buildings, especially those in the rural districts, are in wretched condition. There is little supervision and little effort to improve the schools or adapt their efforts to the needs of the community. The reports of the State Departments of Georgia and Alabama indicate that 70 per cent of the colored teachers have third grade or temporary certificates, representing a preparation less than that usually given in the first eight elementary grades. Investigations made by supervisors of colored schools in other States indicate that the percentage of poorly prepared colored teachers is almost as high in the other southern States.

The supervisor of white elementary rural schools in one of the States recently wrote concerning negro schools: "I never visit one of these (negro) schools without feeling that we are wasting a large part of this money and are neglecting a great opportunity. The negro schoolhouses are miserable beyond all description. They are usually without comfort, equipment, proper lighting or sanitation. Nearly all of the negroes of school age in the district are crowded into these miserable structures during the short term which the school runs. Most of the teachers are absolutely untrained and have been given certificates by the county board, not because they have passed the examination, but because it is necessary to have some kind of negro teacher. Among the negro rural schools which I have visited, I have found only one in which the highest class knew the multiplication table."

The treatment which the negroes received at the hands of the courts and the guardians of the peace constituted another cause of the migration. Negroes largely distrust the courts and have to depend on the influence of their aristocratic white friends. When a white man assaults a negro he is not punished. When a white man kills a negro he is usually freed without extended legal proceedings, but the rule as laid down by the southern judge is usually that when a negro kills a white man, whether or not in self-defense, the negro must die. Negro witnesses count for nothing except when testifying against members of their own race. The testimony of a white man is conclusive in every instance. In no State of the South can a negro woman get a verdict for seduction, nor in most cases enter a suit against a white man; nor, where a white man is concerned, is the law of consent made to apply to a negro girl.

It will be said, however, that such drastic action is not general in the South; but throughout the Black Belt the negroes suffer from arrests and impositions for petty offenses which make their lives sometimes miserable. The large number of negroes owning automobiles is a source of many conflicts. Many collisions, possibly avoidable, have resulted in wresting from the negroes concerned excessive damages which go to increase the returns of the courts. For example, the chauffeur of one of the most influential negroes in Mississippi collided with a white man's car. Although there was sufficient evidence to exonerate the chauffeur concerned, the owner of the vehicle was forced to pay damages and sell his car.[1]

In the Birmingham district of Alabama a striking discrimination is made in the arrests for failure to pay the street tax. Mr. Henry L. Badham, President of the Bessemer Coal, Iron and Land Company, said in commenting on the causes of the migration:

I do not blame the negroes for going away from Birmingham. The treatment that these unfortunate negroes are receiving from the police is enough to make them desire to depart. The newspapers have printed articles about the departure of the laborers from Birmingham. On one page there is a story to the effect that something should be done to prevent the exodus of the negroes to other cities. And then on the same page there appears a little paragraph stating that negroes were arrested for failure to pay $2.50 street tax. The injustice of arresting these negroes for the inability to have $2.50 ready to turn over into the coffers of the city is obvious. While they have been taken into custody, despite their protests that they merely have not a sufficient amount of money with which to meet the demand, you do not see that white men are arrested for the failure to pay the tax. There is no gainsaying the fact that there are thousands of men walking the streets who have not paid a similar sum into the treasury of the city. The negroes ought to get a square deal. When he is without funds, you can not blame him for that. The city police ought to be more reliable, or at least show no favoritism.[2]

The fee system in the courts of the South is one of the most effective causes of the migration. The employers of labor fought this system for eight years and finally got it abolished in Jefferson county, Alabama. Under this system the sheriff

[1] Work and Johnson. *Report on the Migration during the World War.*
[2] *Montgomery Advertiser.*

received a fee for feeding all prisoners. The greater the number of prisoners, the greater would be the income for the sheriff's office. As a result, it became customary in Jefferson county, Alabama, to arrest negroes in large numbers. Deputy sheriffs would go out to mining camps where there were large numbers of laborers and bring back fifty or more negroes at a time. This condition became unbearable both to the employer and to the employe. Calling attention to the evil of this fee system, Dr. W. H. Oates, State Prison Inspector, said in his annual report for 1914: [1]

The vile, pernicious, pervading fee system beggars description and my vocabulary is inadequate to describe its deleterious and baneful effects. It increases in the management of our jails greed for the almighty dollar. Prisoners are arrested because of the dollar and, shame to say, are frequently kept in captivity for months in steel cages for no other reason than the almighty dollar.

During the fiscal year ending September 30, 1917, Jefferson county had 6,000 prisoners as follows:

In jail at the beginning of the year....................328
Incarcerated during the year:
     White men 1,289
     Negro men 3,636
     White women 118
     Negro women 969
                           ———
       Total 6,340

The fee bill, according to the sheriff's annual report of this department was $37,688.90. As the law provided that for each prisoner the sheriff shall receive 30 cents a day for feeding, and as a matter of fact the sheriff fed them for 10 cents a day, it is clear that he made a net profit of $25,125.94 during one fiscal year or at the same rate for his term of four years, $100,503.76. [2]

Another frequent complaint was directed against the accommodations for travel. It generally happens that the cars are crowded because the amount of space allotted is insufficient, and

[1] Annual Report of the Prison Inspector of Alabama, 1914.
[2] Report of the Sheriff of Jefferson County, Alabama, 1917.

negroes as a class are denied accommodation in sleeping and dining cars. Usually there is but one toilet for both sexes and the waiting rooms at stations are cut off, unclean and insanitary. Then there are numerous petty offenses, which in themselves appear trifling, but which are spoken of as being on the whole considerably annoying. White men are permitted to come into the negroes' part of the coach and entertain the conductor, newsboy and flagman, all of whom usually make their headquarters there. The drunkards, the insane and other undesirables are forced into this comparment among negro women who have to listen to oaths and vulgar utterances. In stopping at some points, the trains halt the negro car in muddy and abominably disagreeable places; the rudeness and incivility of the public servants are ever apparent, and at the stations the negroes must wait at a separate window until every white passenger has purchased a ticket before he is waited on, although he may be delayed long enough to miss the train.

Both whites and negroes in mentioning the reasons for the movement generally give lynching as one of the most important causes and state that the fear of the mob has greatly accelerated the exodus. Negroes in Florida gave as their reason for going north the horrible lynchings in Tennessee. The white press in Georgia maintained that lynchings were driving the negroes in large numbers from that State. A careful study of the movement, however, shows that bad treatment by representatives of the law caused almost as many negroes to leave the South as lynchings, for, whereas lynchings were more or less sporadic, persecutions and mistreatment by representatives of the law were trials which all negroes had continually to bear and from which they were anxious to escape.[1]

Many of these causes then have their origin on the one hand in the attitude which the South assumes toward the negro as expressed in law and public opinion, and on the other hand in the feeling of the negro toward the South because of the treatment given him. A negro educator of Mississippi sought to explain the situation, saying:

[1] Work and Johnson, *Report on the Migration during the World War.*

Many white men of high intellectual ability and keen discernment have mistaken the negroes' silence for contentment, his facial expression for satisfaction at prevailing conditions, and his songs and jovial air for happiness.[1] But this is not always so. These are his methods of bearing trouble and keeping his soul sweet under seeming wrongs. In the absence of a spokesman or means of communication with the whites over imagined grievances, he has brightened his countenance, smiled and sung to ease his mind. In the midst of it all he is unable to harmonize with the practices of daily life the teachings of the Bible which the white Christian placed in his hands. He finds it difficult to harmonize the fatherhood of God and the brotherhood of man, and his faith is put to the test in the *Providence* which enslaved his ancestors, corrupted his blood and placed upon him stigmas more damaging than to be a leper or convict by making his color a badge of infamy and his preordained social position at the bottom of human society. So firmly has his status been fixed by this *Providence* that neither moral worth, fidelity to trust, love of home, loyalty to country, or faith in God can raise him to human recognition.

When he remembers that he has been the beast of burden of southern civilization and the foundation of its luxuriant ease, when he rehearses to his children that he was the South's sole dependence when his master was away repelling hostile armies, and how he worked by day and guarded his unprotected mistress and her children at night, or accompanied his master to the swamps of Virginia and the Carolinas and bound up his wounds or brought his maimed or dead body home on his shoulders, these children can not understand the attitude of the South toward them. They do not understand why they have not been educated to efficiency and employed to the best interest of the South. They do not understand why they have not been given better living conditions, a more equitable division of funds appropriated for the education of the youth, nor provisions made for their higher or professional training, or why so much prejudice is engendered in the practice of these professions among their own people. They do not understand why they have been made to toil at starvation wages and to pay heavy fines and suffer long prison sentences for stealing food and clothing. They do not understand why no estimate is placed upon negro virtue and the full rights of citizenship are denied to negroes of education, character and worth. If some mysterious *Providence* has ordained that they support themselves and employers by farming, they do not understand why they are deprived of agricultural schools. They do not see why mere prejudice would prevent them from obtaining a square deal when contending for the

[1] Mr. Charles S. Johnson reports the following from Mississippi:
"The police of most of the cities are rough and indiscriminate in their treatment of negroes. At the depot during the summer, on several occasions, negro porters were severely beaten by policemen for trivial reasons. This, it was said, started a stream of young men that cleaned the town of porters.
"Fee constables made their living from arresting negroes, indiscriminately, on trivial charges. A white man, to whom a prominent negro physician had gone for advice on a case concerning his arrest on a charge of having no lights on his automobile, said, 'If I were a negro, I would rather appear before a Russian court than come before a court here for trial.'"

possessions of life, liberty and property. They do not understand why they are not protected from petty peace officers in search of fees and from mobs while in the hands of officers of the law. Finally, they do not understand why there is so little genuine sympathy and brotherhood between them and the only people they know—the people whose language and customs they use, under whose laws they live, whose Bible they read, whose God they serve. These thoughts possessed the negroes' mind when, twelve months ago, the boll weevil and rains destroyed the crops in the South and the European war was calling foreigners from field and factory in the North.[1]

One should bear in mind that the two generations of negroes living in the South are affected differently by the measures of control of the whites, and in many cases respond differently to treatment received. The older generation of whites and blacks avoided much friction by a sort of mutual understanding. The children of colored and white parents come less frequently into friendly contact and find it difficult to live together on the terms accepted by their fathers. Negro parents appreciate this situation but, although admitting that they can tolerate the position to which they are assigned, they do not welcome such an arrangement for their children. For this reason they are not reluctant to send their sons away from home. Should the children remain there, they live in a state of anxiety for their safety. They would not have them grow up as they, encompassed by restraints, and the young men themselves appear to entertain toward the prevailing system a more aggressive hostility.

A woman of color in Greenville, Mississippi, for example, had a son in a northern State and was afraid to invite him home to pay a visit because, as she stated, " for him to accept the same abuses to which we, his parents, are accustomed, would make him much less than the man we would have him be." Another negro, a physician, the " Nestor " of his profession, having practiced in his State over thirty-five years, said:

Sir, I can't expect my son to accept the treatment under which I have been brought up. My length of residence here and the number of friends whom I know of the older and more aristocratic type of whites will protect

[1] Work and Johnson, *Report on the Migration during the World War.*

me, but as for him, there is no friendship. Now, as for me, there is no reason why I should leave. I am making as much money as I could anywhere else and all of the white people respect me. But I am just one out of a thousand. The younger men have neither my contact nor influence.

A lawyer of remarkable talent formerly of Mississippi, now living with his children in Chicago, who had felt keenly this humiliation and recognized it as one of the motives behind his change of residence, thus stated the situation:

One peculiar phase of the white southern prejudice is that no matter how well liked or popular a colored man be in any community, his son does not share that popularity unless he enters a field of endeavor distinctly lower in the scale than that occupied by his parent. My experience goes both ways on this subject. My stepfather was a dearly beloved colored man of the old school, but when he sent me off to Oberlin College I returned to find that the community in which I had been beloved as a boy in attendance at the rude country school looked at me askance. It took twenty years to overcome the handicap of attempting to occupy a higher sphere than that to which the community thought it right to assign me. My experiences were repeated by my son. He was a well liked boy by the best people in a city of about twenty-five thousand, because he was my son and was polite and agreeable. When he went to a nearby Mississippi college and worked in his summer vacations in a local industrial plant, they still thought well of him, but when it was learned that he was being graduated at Oberlin College, and his picture appeared in a college year book, among others, my intimate white friends wanted to know the necessity for so much education and, with a shrug of the shoulder, they let all mention of him drop, as if he had offended the most sacred laws of the community. This spirit appeared so marked that I did not have him come back to visit his mother and me during the summer vacation. I have seen the same spirit in many instances. No man can explain why it is, but it is so.[1]

[1] Work and Johnson, *Report on the Migration during the World War.*

CHAPTER III

Stimulation of the Movement

It is not surprising that the exodus grew so contagious when viewed in the light of the numerous factors which played a part in influencing its extension. Considering the temper of the South and its attitude toward any attempt to reduce its labor supply, it is readily apparent that leaders who openly encouraged the exodus would be in personal danger. There were, of course, some few who did venture to voice their belief in it, but they were in most cases speedily silenced. A Methodist minister was sent to jail because he was said to have been enticing laborers to go north and work for a New York firm, which would give employment to fifty of his people. The tactics adopted by influential persons who favored the movement, therefore, were of necessity covert and very much guarded.

One of the chief stimuli was discussion. The very fact that negroes were leaving in large numbers was a disturbing factor. The talk in the barber shops and grocery stores where men were wont to assemble soon began to take the form of reasons for leaving. There it was the custom to review all the instances of mistreatment and injustice which fell to the lot of the negro in the South. It was here also that letters from the North were read and fresh news on the exodus was first given out. In Hattiesburg, Mississippi, it was stated that for a while there was no subject of discussion but the migration. " The packing houses in Chicago for a while seemed to be everything," said one negro. " You could not rest in your bed at night for Chicago." Chicago came to be so common a word that they began to call it " Chi." Men went down to talk with the Chicago porters on the Gulf and Ship Island Railroad which ran

26

through the town. They asked questions about the weather in Chicago. The report was that it was the same as in Hattiesburg.[1] In every circle the advisability of leaving was debated. In the churches the pastors, seeing their flocks leaving, at first attempted to dissuade them. The people refused to come to church. In the church meetings there were verbal clashes on the matter of the attitude toward the migration. Some few had been careful enough to go north and investigate for themselves and friends. A man learned of the North through a friend whose relatives wrote him from that section. He, thereupon, decided to pay a visit of two weeks, going in August. The attitude of the North overwhelmed him. At Fulton, Kentucky, while he was on the train a white man was sitting in front of him. He wanted to ask him a question but hesitated fearing that he would be rebuffed. He finally addressed the stranger, who answered him courteously and kindly, calling his attention to other points of interest in the North. At Gary, Indiana, he met a gentleman who said he had been mayor of Gary for seven years. He described the Gary school system and promised him an education for his children. He was assured employment at $4 a day for eight hours' work.[2]

A still more powerful, though insidious factor, was the work of public speakers who hid their intentions behind their unique method of presentation. In a lecture on the question of migration a speaker, who is a widely known character, made these remarks:

So many of my folks are leaving that I thought I'd go up and see whether or not they had made a mistake. I found thousands of old friends up there making more money than they'd ever made in their lives. I said to one woman in Chicago, "Well, Sister ——, I see you're here." "Yes, Brother ——, I'm here, thank the Lord." "Do you find it any colder up here than it was in Mississippi?" "Did I understand you correctly to say cold? Honey, I mean it's cold. It is *some* cold." "But you expect to return, don't you?" "Don't play with me, chile. What am I going to return for? I should say not. Up here you see when I come out on the street I walk on nice smooth pavements. Down home I got to walk home through the mud. Up here at nights it don't matter much about coming

[1] Johnson, *Report on the Migration from Mississippi.*
[2] *Ibid.*

home from church. Down home on my street there ain't a single lamp post. And say, honey, I got a bath tub!"[1]

He related the instance of his visit to an automobile plant where he was met at the door by a " stalwart, handsome, six-footer as black as midnight." He asked his companion the name of this "potentate." He was told that this man was an experienced machinist. Every car that passed out of that plant must have his O. K. He added further that his salary was something like $100 a week and that the incident showed the unlimited chance for expansion in the North. When he began to enumerate some of the positions which "men of the race" were holding, the audience became enthusiastic beyond control. One man in the audience, who had been to Detroit, could restrain himself no longer and stood up to inform the audience that there were also colored street car conductors and motormen and that he had seen them with his own eyes. The speaker paid no attention to this interruption and the audience appeared not to notice it, but began to exchange reports among themselves. The speaker added that he had found negroes in the North, well dressed and looking like men—for the first time in their lives—men who were simply "bums" at home. In excusing the indisposition of some negroes toward work, he said, "How in the world can you expect a man to work faithfully all day long for fifty cents?"[2]

Among the important stimuli were the rumors in circulation. When a community is wrought up, it is less difficult to believe remarkable tales. To persons beyond the influence of this excitement it is somewhat difficult to conceive how the rumor that the Germans were on their way through Texas to take the southern States could have been believed. And yet it is reported that this extravagant fiction was taken seriously in some quarters. On the outskirts of Meridian, Mississippi, a band of gypsies was encamped. The rumor gained circulation that the Indians were coming back to retake their land lost years ago. It was further rumored that the United States Government

---

[1] Johnson, *Report on the Migration from Mississippi.*
[2] *Ibid.*

was beginning a scheme to transport all negroes from the South to break up the Black Belt. Passed from mouth to mouth, unrestrainedly these reports became verïties.

It was further asserted on the word and honor " of one in position to know " that the Chicago packing houses needed and would get fifty thousand negroes before the end of the year. One explanation of the belief that the South was overrun with labor agents was the fact that every strange face came to be recognized as a man from the North looking for laborers. If he denied it, they simply thought he was concealing his identity from the police, and if he said nothing, his silence was regarded as sufficient affirmation. Hundreds of disappointments are to be traced to the rumor that a train would leave on a certain date. Hundreds would come to the station prepared to leave and, when no agent appeared, purchased their own tickets.

The questions of wages and privileges were grossly featured. Some men, on being questioned, supposed that it was possible for every common laborer to receive from $4 to $10 a day, and that $50 a week was not an unusual wage. The strength of this belief has been remarked by several social agencies in the North which attempted to supply the immigrants with work. The actual wages paid, though much in excess of those they had been receiving, were often disappointing. Similarly in the matter of privilege and " rights " it was later revealed that unbounded liberty was not to be found in the North. The singular cases of misconduct, against which the more sober minded preached, possibly had their root in the beautiful and one-sided pictures of the North which came to the South.

The *Chicago Defender,* a weekly negro newspaper, with its pronounced radical utterances, its criticism of the South, its policy of retaliation, etc., contributed greatly to the exodus.[1]

---

[1] Some of the material prepared by the *Defender* for consumption in the South was as follows:

" Turn a deaf ear to everybody. You see they are not lifting their laws to help you, are they? Have they stopped their Jim Crow cars? Can you buy a Pullman sleeper where you wish? Will they give you a square deal in court yet? When a girl is sent to prison she becomes the mistress of the guards and others in authority, and women prisoners are put on the streets to work—something they don't do to a white woman. And our leaders

Its influence can be imagined when, after reading the southern white papers with only occasional references to the negroes which might be called commendable and numerous articles which were for the most part distasteful, negroes could read the things they wanted to hear most, expressed in a manner in which they would not dare express them. It voiced the unexpressed thoughts of many and made accusations for which they themselves would have been severely handled. Freud's theory of the suppressed wish finds a happy illustration in this rage over the *Chicago Defender*. Expressed in terms of figures, the circulation of the paper at the beginning of the movement was something like 50,000. In 1918 it had grown to 125,000. It had a large circulation in Mississippi and the supply was usually bought up on the first day of its arrival. Copies were passed around until worn out. One prominent negro asserted that "negroes grab the *Defender* like a hungry mule grabs fodder." In Gulfport, Mississippi, a man was regarded "intelligent" if he read the *Defender*. It was said that in Laurel, Mississippi, old men who did not know how to read would buy it because it was regarded as precious.

It was this paper that named the exodus "The Great Northern Drive," and set the date May 15th, announced the arrivals and took responsibility for inducing "the poor brethren" from the South. It was accused of ruining Hattiesburg, Mississippi, by promoting this rush to the North. The sale of this paper was, therefore, forbidden in several towns in the South. A correspondent said: "White people are paying more attention to the race in order to keep them in the South, but the *Chicago Defender* has emblazoned upon their minds 'Bound for the Promised Land.'"

will tell you the South is the best place for you. Turn a deaf ear to the scoundrel, and let him stay. Above all, see to it that that jumping-jack preacher is left in the South, for he means you no good here in the North. . . . Once upon a time we permitted other people to think for us— today we are thinking and acting for ourselves, with the result that our 'friends' are getting alarmed at our progress. We'd like to oblige these unselfish (?) souls and remain slaves in the South; but to other sections of the country we have said, as the song goes, 'I hear you calling me,' and have boarded the train, singing, 'Good-bye, Dixie Land.'"

In answer to the warnings of the South against the rigors of the northern winters, the *Defender* said:

To die from the bite of frost is far more glorious than at the hands of a mob. I beg you, my brother, to leave the benighted land. You are a free man. Show the world that you will not let false leaders lead you. Your neck has been in the yoke. Will you continue to keep it there because some " white folks' nigger " wants you to? Leave for all quarters of the globe. Get out of the South. Your being there in the numbers in which you are gives the southern politician too strong a hold on your progress. . . . So much has been said through the white papers in the South about the members of the race freezing to death in the North. They .freeze to death down South when they don't take care of themselves. There is no reason for any human being staying in the Southland on this bugaboo handed out by the white press.[1]

If you can freeze to death in the North and be free, why freeze to death in the South and be a slave, where your mother, sister and daughter are raped and burned at the stake; where your father, brother and sons are treated with contempt and hung to a pole, riddled with bullets at the least mention that he does not like the way he is treated. Come North then, all you folks, both good and bad. If you don't behave yourselves up here, the jails will certainly make you wish you had. For the hard-working man there is plenty of work—if you really want it. The *Defender* says come.[2]

---

[1] The following clippings are taken from these white papers:
" Aged Negro Frozen to Death—Albany, Ga., February 8.
" Yesterday the dead body of Peter Crowder, an old negro, was found in an out-of-the-way place where he had been frozen to death during the recent cold snap."—*Macon Telegraph*.
" Dies from Exposure—Spartanburg, S. C., February 6.
" Marshall Jackson, a negro man, who lived on the farm of J. T. Harris near Campobello, Sunday night froze to death."—*South Carolina State*.
" Negro Frozen to Death in Fireless Gretna Hut.
" Coldest weather in the last four years claimed a victim Friday night, when Archie Williams, a negro, was frozen to death in his bed in a little hut in the outskirts of Gretna."—*New Orleans Item*, February 4.
" Negro Woman Frozen to Death Monday.
" Harriet Tolbert, an aged negro woman, was frozen to death in her home at 18 Garibaldi Street early Monday morning during the severe cold."—*Atlanta Constitution*, February 6.
[2] Articles such as the following kept alive the spirit of the exodus:
" Tampa, Florida, January 19. J. T. King, supposed to be a race leader, is using his wits to get on the good side of the white people by calling a meeting to urge our people not to migrate north. King has been termed a ' good nigger ' by his pernicious activity on the emigration question. Reports have been received here that all who have gone north are at work and pleased with the splendid conditions in the North. It is known here that in the North there is a scarcity of labor; mills and factories are open to them. People are not paying any attention to King and are packing and ready to travel north to the '·promised land.'"
" Jackson, Miss., March 23. J. H. Thomas, Birmingham, Alabama, Brownsville Colony, has been here several weeks and is very much pleased with

The idea that the South is a bad place, unfit for the habitation of colored folk, was duly emphasized. Conditions most distasteful to negroes were exaggerated and given first prominence. In this the *Defender* had a clear field, for the local colored newspapers dared not make such unrestrained utterances.[1]   In

the North. He is working at the Pullman Shops, making twice as much as he did at home. Mr. Thomas says the 'exodus' will be greater later on in the year, that he did not find four feet of snow or would freeze to death. He lives at 346 East Thirty-fifth St."

" Huntsville, Alabama, January 19. Fifteen families, all members of the race, left here today for Pittsburgh, Pa., where they will take positions as butlers and maids, getting sixty to seventy-five dollars a month against fifteen and twenty paid here. Most of them claim that they have letters from their friends who went early and made good saying that there was plenty of work, and this field of labor is short owing to the vast amount of men having gone to Europe and not returned."

" Shreveport, La., April 13. The Business Men's League held a meeting here and the white daily papers reported that it was for the purpose of discouraging people from going north. The meeting had no such object. On the other hand, members of the race claim that on May 15th they will be found leaving with the great northern drive."

" The northern invasion has already started, much earlier than predicted. Many members of the race refused to wait until spring. They have started despite the snow and cold. Last week thirty-one came here from Hattiesburg, Mississippi, and said they intended to stay. They were well clothed, having heavy overcoats and rubber overshoes."

" Memphis, Tenn., June 1. Your correspondent took a walk to Central station Saturday night just to see what was going on, and to his surprise and delight, he saw gathered there between 1,500 and 2,000 race men and women. Number 4, due to leave for Chicago at 8:00 o'clock, was held up twenty minutes so that those people who hadn't purchased tickets might be taken aboard. It was necessary to add two additional eighty-foot steel coaches to the Chicago train in order to accommodate the race people, and at the lowest calculation there were more than 1,200 taken aboard."

" St. Louis, Mo., May 11. The *Defender* propaganda to leave sections of the South where they find conditions intolerable is receiving a hearty response. A communication was received by a *Defender* representative last week from Houston, Texas, asking for information relative to conditions in this city and the writer stated a number of persons were planning to leave Houston for this city later on. The information was promptly and cheerfully given."

" Tallulah, La., January 19. This time it's a professor. Heretofore it has been the preachers who have been paid by the white men of the South to tell our people that the North is no place for them. A bigger lie never was uttered. But now it is a professor. He is licking the white man's hand to hold a little $35 job as a backwoods school teacher. He got his name in the papers (white) as 'good nigger.' Just because this 'would-be professor' has been making speeches, asking that our people remain here and be treated like dogs, they are starting a crusade north, and by Easter there will not be one left to tell the tale."

[1] " Forest City, Ark., February 16. David B. Smith (white) is on trial for life for the brutal murder of a member of the race, W. H. Winford, who refused to be whipped like others. This white man had the habit of making his 'slave' submit to this sort of punishment and when Winford

fact, reading the *Chicago Defender* provided a very good substitute for the knowledge which comes through travel. It had the advantage of bringing the North to them. Without fear of exaggeration it is safe to say its policy was successful in inciting thousands of restless negroes to venture north, where they were assured of its protection and the championship of their cause. There are in Chicago migrants who attribute their presence in the North to its encouraging pictures of relief from conditions at home with which they became more and more dissatisfied, as they read.

The setting of a definite date was another stimulus. The great northern drive was scheduled to begin May 15, 1917. This date, or the week following, singularly corresponds with the date of the heaviest rush to the North, the periods of greatest temporary congestion and the awakening of the North to the presence of their guests. Letters to the *Chicago Defender* and to the social agencies in the North informed them that they were preparing to come in the great drive. One of many such letters received is presented.

April 24, 1917.

Mr. R. S. Abbott,
    Editor, the *Chicago Defender,*
Sir:

I have been reading the *Defender* for one year or more, and last February I read about the great northern drive to take place May 15, on Thursday, and now I can hear so many people speaking of an excursion to the North on the 15th of May for $3. My husband is in the North already working, and he wants us to come up in May, so I want to know if it is true about the excursion. I am getting ready and, oh, so many others also, and we want to know is that true so we can be in the drive. So please answer at once. We are getting ready.

Yours,

This was perhaps the most popular date, but there were others, of which August 15 was one. Usually the dates set were for Wednesday and Saturday nights, following pay days.

refused to stand for it, he was whipped to death with a 'black snake' whip. The trial of Smith is attracting very little attention. As a matter of fact, the white people here think nothing of it as the dead man is a 'nigger.' This very act, coupled with other recent outrages that have been heaped upon our people, are causing thousands to leave, not waiting for the great spring movement in May."

Personal appeals in the form of letters have a recognized weight in influencing action. The United States mail was about the most active and efficient labor agent. The manner in which the first negroes left made great opportunities for letter writing. It is to be remembered that the departure of one person was regarded always in the light of an experiment. The understanding existed between a man and his friends that he would honestly inform them of conditions in the North. Letters were passed around and read before large groups. A woman from Hattiesburg is accredited with having sent back a letter which enticed away over 200 persons. A tailor who had settled in a town of white people in the West wrote a letter which was read in a church. It explained the advantages of the free schools open to all, and the privilege to ride and to go where one pleases. The reading of the letter brought forth long and loud applause. A man who had left home, writes back to his friend yet undecided:

Mike, old boy, I was promoted on the first of the month. I was made first assistant to the head carpenter. When he is out of place I take everything in charge and was raised to $95 per month. You know I know my stuff. What's the news generally around H'burg? I should have been here twenty years ago. I just begin to feel like a man. It's a great deal of pleasure in knowing that you have got some privileges. My children are going to the same school with the whites and I don't have to humble to no one. I have registered. Will vote the next election and there isn't any ' yes, sir, and no, sir.' It's all yes and no, and no, Sam, and Bill.

The man has long since been joined by his friend.

The pastor of a Hattiesburg church received a letter from one of his members with the extravagant assertion that the people whose funerals he had preached were in Chicago (meaning Heaven) because they were good Christians. To give assurance on the question of weather migrants in the North would mention the fact that they were writing with their coats off. A fact which strengthened the belief in the almost incredible wages offered in the North was the money sent back to the families in the South. A man whose wife had preceded him wrote that she was making $3.50 a day in charge of a bluing works in Chicago, and actually sent home $15 every two weeks.

A'nother man wrote that he was in Gary working at his trade making sometimes as much as $7 a day. He sent home $30 every two weeks. Fully one-half, or perhaps even more of those who left, did so at the solicitation of friends through correspondence.[1]

Despite the restraints on loose talk in encouragement of the exodus, there were other means of keeping the subject alive. One method, of course, was the circulation of literature from the North. One of the most novel schemes was that of a negro dentist in a southern town who had printed on the reverse side of his business cards quotations from rather positive assertions by northerners on the migration.[2] The northern press

[1] Johnson, *Report on the Migration from Mississippi.*

[2] "There is no class of people and no ethical question that will not feel the effects of the war. The negroes of this country who go to France to fight, or who replace workingmen who go as soldiers will demand, and justly so, full American rights. The United States can not stand before the world as the champion of freedom and democracy and continue to burn men alive and lynch them without fair trial. The National Association for the Advancement of Colored People calls upon this country to 'clear her conscience before she can fight for the world's good,' by abolishing lynching and ceasing all oppression of negroes. This is a national problem and more particularly one of the South. In Europe there are practically no race distinctions. A negro can mix with white folk as an equal, just as a Spaniard, for example, does here; even intermarriage is not regarded as miscegenation. The race problem here is a different matter, however, as even the more intelligent negroes themselves will acknowledge. The negro should be assured all the protection and rights that go with American citizenship, but in this is not involved intermarriage or social equality."— *Leslie's Illustrated Weekly,* October 13, 1917.

"The foreign laborer has been called home to bear arms for his country. The daily death toll and waste and the recently enacted immigration law make it certain that he will not soon return in great numbers. As a result a large market exists for the negro laborer in localities in which he would have been considered an impudent trespasser had he attempted to enter a few years ago. The history of the world from the days of Moses to the present shows that where one race has been subjugated, oppressed or proscribed by another and exists in large numbers, permanent relief has come in one or two ways—amalgamation or migration. The thought of amalgamation is not to be entertained. If conditions in the South for the colored man are to be permanently improved, many of those who now live there should migrate and scatter throughout the North, East and West. I believe the present opportunity providential."—Hon. John C. Ashbury, Philadelphia Bar.

"This is the psychological moment to say to the American white government from every pulpit and platform and through every newspaper, 'Yes, we are loyal and patriotic. Boston Common, Bunker Hill, Gettysburg, Fort Pillow, Appomattox, San Juan Hill and Carrizal will testify to our loyalty. While we love our flag and country, we do not believe in fighting for the protection of commerce on the high seas until the powers that be give us at least some verbal assurance that the property and lives of the members

early welcomed the much needed negro laborers to the North and leaders of thought in that section began to upbraid the South for its antagonistic attitude towards the welfare of the negroes, who at last had learned to seek a more congenial home.

A stronger influence than this, though not quite so frequent, was the returned migrant who was a living example of the prosperity of the North. It was a frequent complaint that these men were as effective as labor agents in urging negro laborers to go north. There are reported numerous instances of men who came to visit their families and returned with thirty to forty men. It has been suspected, and with a strong suggestion of truth, that many of these were supplied with funds for the trip by the northern firms which employed them. A woman whose daughter had gone north had been talking of her daughter's success. The reports were so opposite to the record of the girl at home that they were not taken seriously. Soon, however, the daughter came home with apparently unlimited money and beautiful clothes, and carried her mother back with her. This was sufficient. It was remarked afterwards: " If she can make $2.50 a day as lazy as she was, I know I can make $4." [1]

The labor agents were a very important factor in stimulating the movement. The number at work in the South appears to have been greatly exaggerated. Agents were more active in large cities where their presence was not so conspicuous. It was difficult to discover because of the very guarded manner in which they worked. One, for example, would walk briskly down the street through a group of negroes and, without turn-

of our race are going to be protected on land from Maine to Mississippi.' Let us have the courage to say to the white American people, ' Give us the same rights which you enjoy, and then we will fight by your side with all of our might for every international right on land and sea.' If this kind of talk is not loyalty, then I am disloyal; if this is not patriotism, then I am unpatriotic; if this is treason, then I am a traitor. It is not that I love Cæsar less, but these black Romans more, who have been true to the flag for two hundred and fifty years. It is infinitely more disgraceful and outrageous to hang and burn colored men, boys and women without a trial in the times of peace than it is for Germans in times of war to blow up ships loaded with mules and molasses."—Reverend A. Clayton Powell, New York, N. Y.

[1] Johnson, *Report on the Migration from Mississippi.*

ing his head, would say in a low tone, " Anybody want to go to Chicago, see me." That was sufficient. Many persons were found to remark frequently on the strange silence which negroes *en masse* managed to maintain concerning the movement of the agents. A white man remarked that it was the first time there had ever happened anything about which he could not get full information from some negro. Agents were reported, at one time or another, in every section from which the migrants went. When the vigilance of the authorities restricted their activities they began working through the mails. Many sections were flooded with letters from the North to persons whose names had been obtained from migrants in the North or through a quiet canvass of the community by unobstructed solicitors.[1]

Poems on the migration were also strong stimuli. In some instances arrests of persons circulating them were made. A bit of poetry which received widespread popularity was one called " Bound for the Promised Land." It was said that this piece of poetry was responsible for much trouble. The *Chicago Defender* reported on June 1, 1917, that five young men were arraigned before Judge John E. Schwartz of Savannah, Georgia, for reading poetry. The police contended that they were inciting riot in the city and over Georgia. Two of the men were sent for thirty days to Brown Farm, a place not fit for human beings. Tom Amaca was arrested for having " Bound for the Promised Land," a poem which had been recently published in the *Defender*. J. N. Chisholm and A. P. Walker were arrested there because they were said to be the instigators.[2] Another very popular poem widely circulated was entitled " Farewell! We're Good and Gone." It was said that this poem influenced thousands to go. Other poems on the migration were " Northward Bound," " The Land of Hope " and " Negro Migration " and " The Reason Why."

[1] Work and Johnson, *Report on the Migration during the World War.*
[2] *Ibid.*

CHAPTER IV

The Spread of the Movement

In the first communities visited by representatives of northern capital, their offers created unprecedented commotion. Drivers and teamsters left their wagons standing in the street. Workers, returning home, scrambled aboard the trains for the North without notifying their employers or their families. The crowds that blackened the pool rooms and "hangouts" faded away as the trains continued to leave. Wild rumors about the North crept into circulation and received unquestioning credence. Songs about Pennsylvania, the spontaneous expression of anxiety and joy over the sudden revelation of a new world, floated about on the lips of the children. Homes were thrown on the market and sold at ruinously low prices.

It was observed that the beginnings in each new community exhibited the same characteristics. This is due in part to a pretty universal state of unrest among negroes throughout the South. Although the first State entered by representatives of northern capital was Florida, their efforts were not confined to that commonwealth. And again, although the Pennsylvania and Erie Railroads were the first to import negroes in large numbers, they were not alone in the field very long. The steel mills of the East and the railroads of the West soon followed—each selecting States from which egress was easy and convenient. The authorities of the cities of Florida, when they began to engage themselves in the suppression of recruiting agents, succeeded in scattering them to other fields where their mere presence, preceded as it was by the news of their mission in the South, was sufficient to attract, first, all of the landless labor, then to loosen the steady workman wedded to the soil, and finally to carry away the best of the working classes. Quite naturally southeastern Georgia was the second district to feel the drain of the exodus. These workers were carried into Pennsylvania, New York and New Jersey for the maintenance work of the roads. North Carolina was next entered; then finally Virginia which had been sending many negroes into New York, Pennsylvania and New Jersey for a number of years.[1]

Numerous illustrations show the popular state of mind at the beginning, when every one was feverish. Men would loudly decry the folly of breaking up their homes, the result of years of unrelenting toil, and venturing into the unknown North, and within less than twenty-four hours, would leave themselves. A good citizen would talk with another about the apparent insanity of those negroes who had " contracted the northern fever." They would condemn their acts with their strongest words. Hardly before another day could pass, one of the two would disappear, having imitated the recklessness of the very people he had so recently condemned.

One man in telling of how they acted, asserts " You could see a man today and he would be calling the people who were leaving all kinds of names; he could even beat you when it came to calling them fools for going north. The next day when you met him he wouldn't talk so loud and the next day he wouldn't let you see him. That would be the last of him, because, unless you went to the depot, you wouldn't see him again. Whenever I saw them shying off from me, I always knew what they had up their sleeves." It was " just naturally fashionable " to leave for the North. A man would make up his mind to go and proceed forthwith to persuade his friends. If they refused, they no longer had any interests in common. In talking with a man who had persistently refused to leave, he declared that he had lost practically every friend he had, simply because he did not agree with them on " the northern question." For the pastors of churches it was a most trying ordeal. They must watch their congregations melt away and could say nothing. If they spoke in favor of the movement, they were in danger of a clash with the authorities. If they

[1] Work, *Report on the Migration from Florida.*

discouraged it, they were accused of being bought up to hold negroes in bondage. If a pastor attempted to persuade negroes to stay, his congregation and his collection would be cut down and in some cases his resignation demanded. In some of the smaller communities the pastors settled this difficulty by following their flock, as was the case of three who left Hattiesburg, Mississippi, following their congregations. Two lumber companies in Mississippi employed a negro to lecture for the purpose of discouraging the exodus. He was handsomely paid, but he was unheeded. Even now he is held in contempt by his former friends.

The devout and religious saw God in the movement. It was inspired, they said, else why could so many thousand negroes all be obsessed at once with the same impulse. There were set afloat rumors that a great calamity was about to befall the Southland. In Georgia and Alabama, hundreds believed that God had cursed the land when he sent droughts and floods and destructive pests to visit them. The number of negroes needed in the North was counted in millions; the wages offered were fabulous and the letters that came from the vanguard painted pictures of a land of plenty. From some communities a small group would leave, promising to inform those behind of the actual state of affairs. For a week or more there would follow a tense period of "watchful waiting" and never ending anxiety, when finally there would arrive a card bearing the terse report "Everything pritty," or "Home ain't nothing like this." On this assurance, a reckless disposition of household effects would follow.[1]

The towns quite naturally were the first to feel the effect. There, the pass rider—the labor agent—could move about more freely. People lived in closer contact and news circulated more rapidly; the papers came in regularly and the negroes themselves could see those leaving. On market days when the country folk reached town they got their first impulse from the commotion. Young country boys failed to return to quiet isolation, and sturdy sensible farmers whose whole lives had been spent on

[1] Work and Johnson, *Report on the Migration during the World War.*

the farm, could not resist the temptation. As they returned they informed their neighbors, saying: " They are leaving town by the thousands," or " Man, colored folks are leaving in droves for the North." There are cases of men who left their fields half plowed and journeyed to the city and thence to the North. In other communities, the beginning would be a timid dribble to the larger cities or directly to the North.[1]

The state of mind of the community under the influence of the first effects of the " fever " is illustrated in authenticated accounts of persons who witnessed the exodus from different cities:

The most interesting thing is how these people left. They were selling out everything they had or in a manner giving it away; selling their homes, mules, horses, cows, and everything about them but their trunks. All around in the country, people who were so old they could not very well get about were leaving. Some left with six to eight very small children and babies half clothed, no shoes on their feet, hungry, not anything to eat and not even a cent over their train fare. Some would go to the station and wait there three or four days for an agent who was carrying them on passes. Others of this city would go in clubs of fifty and a hundred at a time in order to get reduced rates. They usually left on Wednesday and Saturday nights. One Wednesday night I went to the station to see a friend of mine who was leaving. I could not get in the station, there were so many people turning like bees in a hive. Officers would go up and down the tracks trying to keep the people back. One old lady and man had gotten on the train. They were patting their feet and singing and a man standing nearby asked, " Uncle, where are you going?" The old man replied, " Well, son, I'm gwine to the promised land."[2]

[1] *The Chicago Defender,* 1916, 1917.
[2] " Whether he knew what he was going for or not," says one, " he did not take time to consider. The slogan was 'going north.' Some never questioned the whys or wherefores but went; led as if, by some mysterious unseen hand which was compelling them on, they just couldn't stay. One old negro when asked why he was leaving, replied: 'I don't know why or where I'm going, but I'm on my way.' The northern fever was just simply contagious; they couldn't help themselves. So far as I know, and I think I am about right, this fever started in and around the vicinity of Bessemer, Alabama. One little village, especially, there was owned by a white man from my home who had gone there the year before carrying some negroes with him. The negroes started leaving this village so fast that he wouldn't allow any more tickets to be sold in this village, but the negroes only scoffed at this. They left the plantations at night and went to other villages for tickets. The fever had now begun and, like all other contagious diseases, it soon spread. I arrived home on May 4 and found my native town all in a bustle. Now, what was it all about? The next club for the North was leaving on May 18. The second-hand furniture store and junk shop were practically overflowing. People were selling out valuable furniture such as whole bedroom sets for only $2. One family that I knew myself sold a

" When the laboring man got paid off," said a Jackson, Mississippi, man, " he bought himself a suit of overalls and a paper valise and disappeared." Even the young married women refused to wait any longer than the time required to save railroad fare. It's strange that when a negro got a notion to leave and he could not sell or give away, he simply locked up his house and left the key with his neighbor. Families with $1,000 worth of furniture have been known to sell it for $150. A negro in Jackson was buying a $1,000 house, on which he had paid $700. When the " fever " struck the town, he sold it for $100 and left.

There was related this instance of a number of negro laborers:

On a plantation in south Georgia, where fifteen or more families were farming as tenants, there had been a great deal of confusion and suffering among the people because of the lack of sufficient food and clothing. There were the Joneses, a family of nine, the Harrisons, a family of ten, and the Battles, a family of six. No family on the place had an allowance of more than $25 per month for food and clothing. When this allowance gave out, nothing could be gotten until the next month and the tenants dared not leave their farms to work elsewhere. The owner of this plantation lived in town ten miles away and only visited the farm about once a week. Much to his surprise, on one of his weekly visits, he found all the homes and farms deserted except one. On that were two old men, Uncle Ben and Uncle Joe, who had been left behind because they were unable to secure passes. Uncle Ben and Uncle Joe sorrowfully told the landlord all that had

---

beautiful expensive home for only $100. In fact people almost gave away their houses and furnishings. Finally, the night for the club to leave came and the crowds at the train were so large that the policemen had to just force them back in order to allow the people to get on and off. After the train was filled with as many people as it could hold, the old engine gave one or two puffs and pulled out, bound for the promised land."

" A very close neighbor of ours," says one, " left for the North. He had a very small family. He left because his youngest son, who had been north a few months, came home with a considerable amount of money which he had saved while on his trip. The father made haste and sold all he had. His son got him a pass. He said it was far better for him to be in the North where he could stand up like a man and demand his rights; so he is there. His daughter Mary remained at home for some time after the family had gone. She finally wrote her father to send her a pass, which he did. She had a small boy that was given her. She was not able to take him and care for him as she would like. Her next door neighbor, a very fine woman who had no children, wanted a child so Mary gave it to her. To secure better wages and more freedom his oldest son went to East St. Louis and remained there until June. Then he left for Chicago. This family sold their chickens and rented their cattle to some of the people in that community."—Work and Johnson, *Report on the Migration during the World War.*

happened, emphasizing the fact that they were the only ones who had remained loyal to him. Then they told him their needs. The landlord, thinking that the old negroes were so faithful, rewarded them with a good sum of money and left with the assurance that they would see to the crops being worked. No sooner had the landlord left than these old men with grips packed and with the money they had received, boarded the train to join their companions in the North.[1]

As an example of the irresistible force which characterized the movement, one old negro made the remark: " I sorter wanted to go myself. I didn't know just where I wanted to go. I just wanted to git away with the rest of them." A woman in speaking of the torture of solitude which she experienced after the first wave passed over her town, said: " You could go out on the street and count on your fingers all the colored people you saw during the entire day. Now and then a disconsolate looking Italian storekeeper would come out in the street, look up and down and walk back. It was a sad looking place, and so quiet it gave you the shivers." [2]

In the heat of the excitement families left carrying members dangerously ill. There is reported one interesting case of a family with one of its members sick with pneumonia. As soon as the woman was able to sit up, she was carried away. At St. Louis it was found necessary to stop because of her condition. Finding that she could not recover, they proceeded to Chicago, where she died. Several of the migrants have seen fit to make heroes of themselves by declining to return to the South even on the advice of a physician. Thus, a certain minister is said to have refused to be sent home when his physician had told him there was a possible chance for recovery in his home in the South. He said that he preferred to die and be buried in the North.

By the summer of 1916, the exodus from Florida had grown to such ungovernable bounds that the more stable classes of negroes became unsettled. A body, representing the influential colored citizens of the State, wrote the editor of the *New York Age:* [3]

[1] Work and Johnson, *Report on the Migration during the World War.*
[2] *Ibid.*
[3] *The New York Age,* August 16, 1916.

JACKSONVILLE, FLA., August 10, 1916.

To the Editor of the *Age:*

To be brief, I beg to state that the (————) of this city, in a regular meeting, voted last Monday that I write your paper asking advice on the subject of migration which is large and really alarming to the people of this State, for thousands of people (colored) are leaving this State, going to Pennsylvania, New York, Maryland and New Jersey, where it is stated they are wanted as laborers in various pursuits. In your mind and to your knowledge, do you think it is the best thing for them to do, and are they bettering condition financially, morally and religiously; even in manhood, citizenship, etc. Our ———— has been asked by the white and colored people here to speak in an advisory way, but we decided to remain silent until we can hear from reliable sources in the North and East, and you have been designated as one of the best. So to speak, our city is in a turmoil—in suspense. You have doubtless heard of the great exodus of negroes to the North, and we presume you have given it some thought, and even investigated it. Please give the benefit of your findings and reasons for your conclusion.

Thanking you in advance for a prompt and full reply to the corresponding secretary,   Yours truly,

Corresponding Secretary.

Caught up in the wave of enthusiasm that swept over the South, these migrants could not resist the impulse to leave. The economic loss resulting from their reckless departure expressed in terms of dollars and cents is another story, and probably can never be even approximately estimated. What seems of most interest here is that they were in the frame of mind for leaving. They left as though they were fleeing some curse; they were willing to make almost any sacrifice to obtain a railroad ticket and they left with the intention of staying. What has been described, of course, can not be construed to apply to every one who left. There were those of the business and professional classes who were promoted by other motives than those which impelled the masses of migrants. There were, for example, migrants who in the South had held positions of relatively high standing by virtue of the fact that there do exist two institutional standards, the white and the black. Measured by the requirements of the latter, they stood high in the respect of the community, but when removed to the North they suffered in the rank of their occupation. A college president or even a school teacher had little opportunity in their respective fields in the North. They had, therefore, migrated because deserted by their neighbors they were left with a prospect of a diminishing social importance.

Professional men followed their practice. In Chicago there are at least six lawyers from Mississippi, with practically the same clientele. At the height of the exodus, one of these came to Chicago and secured admission to the bar in order that he might be in a position to move quickly if his practice were too severely cut down. Several physicians of the State have remarked that they would now be in the East or the North if reciprocity with the State of Mississippi were possible.[1] Business men have been reported to have moved North for the sole purpose of collecting debts. Others are cooler and more calculating in preparing to leave. One pharmacist, for instance, plans to move within the next five years. It is true that some of those who came in the movement would have come even if no one else had decided to migrate. The influence of the general state of mind, however, on the great majority is of most concern in determining the forces behind the exodus.

Possibly the numbers to leave the South would have been considerably smaller had there not been existent so universal a readiness to respond to a call in almost any direction. The causes of this state of mind are stated elsewhere. What is important here is the behavior of the persons leaving which exerted such a compelling influence on their neighbors. The actions are illustrative not only of the contagion of the movement, but of the fundamental emotions of the negroes who formed the exodus. Thus it was, for example, that the movement was called the "exodus" from its suggestive resemblance to the flight of the Israelites from Egypt, *The Promised Land, Crossing over Jordan* (the Ohio River), and *Beulah Land*. At times demonstrations took on a rather spectacular aspect, as when a party of 147 from Hattiesburg, Mississippi, while crossing the Ohio River, held solemn ceremonies. These migrants knelt down and prayed; the men stopped their watches and, amid

[1] Johnson, *Report on the Migration from Mississippi.*

tears of joy, sang the familiar songs of deliverance, " I done come out of the Land of Egypt with the good news." The songs following in order were " Beulah Land " and " Dwelling in Beulah Land." One woman of the party declared that she could detect an actual difference in the atmosphere beyond the Ohio River, explaining that it was much lighter and that she could get her breath more easily.[1]

The general direction of the spread of the movement was from east to west. While efforts were being made to check the exodus from Florida, the good citizens of Texas were first beginning to note a stir of unrest in their sections. On the other hand, the march of the boll weevil, that stripped the cotton fields of the South, was from west to east. Where there was wide unemployment, depression and poverty as a result of the great floods in Alabama, the cutting down of the cane area in Louisiana, the boll weevil in Mississippi, there were to be found thousands who needed no other inducement save the prospect of a good job. Indeed, it is alleged by some negroes that the myriads of labor agents who were said to be operating in the South were creatures of the imagination of an affrighted Southland; that but few were actually offering positions in the North; but their success was due to the overpowering desire on the part of the negroes to go.[2]

In September of 1916 a Georgia correspondent of the *Atlanta Constitution* wrote:

For the past two or three weeks I have been receiving two or more letters daily from people in all sections of Georgia asking my advice as to the advisability of the colored people leaving the State in large numbers, as they have been leaving for the past six months. I think it is a mistake for our people to sell and practically give their earnings of years just on a hearsay that they will be given larger salaries and great advantages in some other part of the country.

It will be remembered that the State of South Carolina was not immediately affected. It was not until the discussions bearing on the negro's insecurity and economic state, which accom-

[1] Johnson. *Report on the Migration from Mississippi.*
[2] Work, *Report on the Migration from Alabama.*

panied the exodus in justification of it, had begun to be emphasized as the cause of the movement that a great exodus took place in the State. The principal occasion here was the unfortunate lynching of Anthony Crawford. A negro newspaper with a correspondent in Abbeville said:

The lynching of Anthony Crawford has caused men and women of this State to get up and bodily leave it. The lynching of Mr. Crawford was unwarranted and uncalled for and his treatment was such a disgrace that respectable people are leaving daily. When they begin to leave in the next few weeks like they have planned, this section will go almost into hysterics as some sections of Georgia and Alabama are doing because they are leaving for the North to better their industrial condition. Crawford is said to have been worth $100,000 in property. His wife and five sons have been ordered to leave. Word comes that neighbors are beginning to leave and the number the first of the week reached 1,000. The cry now is—"Go north, where there is some humanity, some justice and fairness." White people have accelerated the movement for the race to move north.

This, however, accounts principally for the spread of the movement as accomplished by northern capital which, hitting the South in spots, made it possible for a wider dissemination of knowledge concerning the North, and actually placed in the North persons with numerous personal connections at home. The husbands and fathers who preceded their families could and did command that they follow, and they in turn influenced their neighbors. It appears that those who came on free transportation were largely men who had no permanent interests or who could afford to venture into strange fields. This indiscriminate method of many of the transporting agencies undoubtedly made it possible for a great number of indigent and thriftless negroes simply to change the scene of their inaction. Yet it is unquestionably true that quite a large proportion of those who went North in this fashion were men honestly seeking remunerative employment, or persons who left through sheer desperation. In the second stage of the movement the club organizations, special parties and chartered cars did most perhaps to depopulate little communities and drain the towns and cities.

This is easily to be accounted for. The free trains, carrying mainly men, were uncertain. They were operated for brief periods in towns, but were in such ill favor with the police that passengers were not safe. The clubs or special parties were worked up by a leader, who was often a woman of influence. She sought her friends and a convenient date was appointed. Arrangements could also be made with friends in the North to receive them. The effectiveness of this method is seen in the fact that neighbor was soliciting neighbor and friend persuading friend. Women in some of the northern cities, joining these clubs, assert that no persuasion was needed; that if a family found that it could not leave with the first groups, it felt desolate and willing to resort to any extremes and sacrifices to get the necessary fare. One woman in a little town in Mississippi, from which over half of the negro population had dribbled away, said: "If I stay here any longer, I'll go wild. Every time I go home I have to pass house after house of all my friends who are in the North and prospering. I've been trying to hold on here and keep my little property. There ain't enough people here I now know to give me a decent burial."

CHAPTER V

The Call of the Self-Sufficient North

A surviving custom of servitude has consigned the mass of negroes to the lower pursuits of labor. Even at this it would be possible to live, for there would be work. In the North, however, such employment has been monopolized by foreign immigrants clearing Ellis Island at the rate of more than a million a year. The usurpation here brought no clash, for the number of negroes in the North scarcely equalled a year's immigration. From the ranks of unskilled labor, accordingly, they were effectively debarred, being used occasionally, and to their own detriment, as strike breakers and forced to receive smaller wages and to make more enemies. From the field of skilled labor they have been similarly debarred by the labor unions.

The labor unions have felt that they had a good case against the negro workman. The complaints most commonly made are that he could be too easily used as a strike breaker and that he lacked interest in the trade union movement. As a matter of fact, both are true. An explanation of this attitude at the same time brings out another barrier opposed by the North to the free access of negroes to trades. Considerable wavering has characterized the attitude of the trade unions toward negro labor. The complexity of their organization makes it difficult to place any responsibility directly for their shortcomings. The fact remains, however, that despite the declaration of the constitution of the federated body that no distinction shall be made on account of sex, color or creed, negroes have been systematically debarred from membership in a great number of labor bodies. Even where there has been no express prohibition in the constitution of local organizations the *disposition* to exclude them has been just as effective. Refused membership, they have easily become strike breakers. The indifference on the part of negroes to the labor movement, however, may well be attributed also to ignorance of its benefits. In a number of cases separate organizations have been granted them.

With the foreign immigration silently crowding him back into the South, the labor unions, the prejudices of his white fellow workman and the paucity of his number making him ineffective as a competitor, driving him from the door of the factory and workshop, the negro workman, whatever his qualifications, was prior to 1914 forced to enter the field of domestic service in the North and farming in the South. The conditions of livelihood in both sections kept him rigidly restricted to this limited economic sphere. In 1910 the total number of negroes ten years of age and over gainfully occupied in the United States was 5,192,535 or 71 per cent of the total number of negroes ten years of age and over. Of this number 2,848,258 or 55.2 per cent were farmers and 1,122,182 or 21.4 per cent were domestic servants. Out of nearly five hundred occupations listed in the census of 1910 three-fourths of the negro working population were limited to two. In the manufacturing and mechanical pursuits throughout the entire United States there were employed scarcely a half million or 12.1 per cent of the working population.

Statistics of labor conditions in certain northern cities support this conclusion. In New York City in 1910, of the negroes ten years of age and over gainfully occupied there were 33,110 males and 26,352 females. Of the males there were engaged in domestic and personal service 16,724 or 47.6 per cent of the total number of males. Of the 26,352 females there were in domestic service 24,647 or 93.5 per cent of the total number. In the occupations which require any degree of skill and utilize the training of acquired trades, the percentage was exceedingly low. For example, in the manufacturing and mechanical pursuits where there were the benefits of labor organizations and higher pay, there were but 4,504 negro males, or 13.6 per cent .of the total number gainfully employed. The per cent of colored women in this line was considerably less. Taken together with the 1,993 dressmakers working outside of factories it was but 8.3 per cent of the total number of females. This line of work, however, as all who are familiar with the manner in which it is done will recognize, is but another form of domestic service. Exclusive of this number the per cent drops to a figure a trifle over one per cent.

Chicago, as another typical northern city, shows practically the same limitations on negro labor. In 1910 there were gainfully employed in this city 27,317 negroes. Of this total 61.8 per cent were engaged in domestic service. The negro women, of course, contributed a larger share to this proportion, theirs being 83.8 per cent of the females ten years of age and over gainfully employed. In the manufacturing and mechanical pursuits there were engaged 3,466 males and 1,038 females, or 18.7 and 1.1 per cent respectively.[1]

Detroit, viewed in the light of its tremendous increase, shows some of the widest differences. In 1910 there were 3,310 negroes of working age profitably employed. Of this number there were but 410 males and 74 females engaged in the manufacturing and mechanical pursuits. Forty-six of the total female working.population were engaged in domestic service. Limited to a few occupations, the negroes naturally encountered there intense competition with the usual result of low wages and numerous other abuses. Whenever they entered new fields, as for instance those designated by the census as trade and transportation, they were generally compelled to accept wages below the standard to obtain such employment.

There appears to have been a slow but steady progress throughout the North toward the accession of negroes to new lines of occupation. This change was forced, unquestionably, by the necessity for seeking new fields even at an economic loss. From the lines of work in which negroes for a long time have held unquestioned prestige, the competition of other nationalities has removed them. It is difficult now to find a barber shop operated by a negro in the business district of any northern city. The most dangerous competitor of the negro in northern industry has been the immigrant, who, unconscious of his subtle

[1] These facts appear in the *United States Census Reports*.

inhibition on the negro's industrial development, crowded him out of employment in the North and fairly well succeeded in holding him in the South. After fifty years of European immigration the foreign born increased from two million to over thirteen million and only five per cent of them have settled in the South. Indeed, the yearly increase in foreign immigration equalled the entire negro population of the North.

The competition in the North has, therefore, been in consequence bitter and unrelenting. Swedes and Germans have replaced negroes in some cities as janitors. Austrians, Frenchmen and Germans have ousted them from the hotels, and Greeks have almost monopolized the bootblacking business. The decline in the domestic service quota of the working negro population, when there has been a decline, seems to have been forced. The figures of the United States census strengthen the belief that the World War has accomplished one of two things: It has either hastened the process of opening up larger fields or it has prevented a serious economic situation which doubtless would have followed the complete supplanting of negroes by foreigners in practically all lines.

Before the war the immigration of foreigners from Europe was proceeding at the enormous rate of over a million a year. This influx was so completely checked by the war that the margin of arrivals over departures for the first three years following the beginning of hostilities was the smallest in fifty years. The following is a statement taken from reports of the Bureau of Foreign Immigration.

IMMIGRATION SINCE 1913

Year	Number
1913	1,197,892
1914	1,218,480
1915	326,700
1916	298,826
1917	295,403

The decrease of over 900,000 immigrants, on whom the industries of the North depended, caused a grave situation. It must be remembered also that of the 295,403 arrivals in 1917, there were included 32,346 English, 24,405 French and 13,350 Scotch who furnish but a small quota of the laboring classes. There were also 16,438 Mexicans who came over the border, and who, for the most part, live and work in the Southwest. The type of immigration which kept prime the labor market of the North and Northwest came in through Ellis Island. Of these, Mr. Frederick C. Howe, Commissioner of Immigration, said that "only enough have come to balance those who have left." He adds further that "As a result, there has been a great shortage of labor in many of our industrial sections that may last as long as the war."

With the establishment of new industries to meet the needs of the war, the erection of munitions plants for the manufacture of war materials and the enlargement of already existing industries to meet the abnormally large demand for materials here and in Europe, there came a shifting in the existing labor supply in the North. There was a rush to the higher paid positions in the munitions plants. This, together with the advancement of the white men to higher positions nearly depleted the ranks of common labor. The companies employing foreign labor for railroad construction work and in the steel mills of Pennsylvania, the tobacco fields of Connecticut, the packing houses, foundries and automobile plants of the Northwest, found it imperative to seek for labor in home fields. The Department of Labor, in the effort to relieve this shortage, through its employment service, at first assisted the migration northward. It later withdrew its assistance when its attention was called to the growing magnitude of the movement and its possible effect on the South.

Deserted by the Department of Labor, certain northern employers undertook to translate their desires into action in 1915, when the anxieties of the New England tobacco planters were felt in the New York labor market. These planters at first rushed to New York and promiscuously gathered up 200 girls of the worst type, who straightway proceeded to demoralize Hartford. The blunder was speedily detected and the employers came back to New York, seeking some agency which might assist them in the solution of their problem.   Importuned for help, the National League on Urban Conditions among Negroes supplied these planters with respectable southern blacks who met this unusual demand for labor in Connecticut.   Later, moreover, it appeared that on the threshold of an unusually promising year the Poles, Lithuanians and Czechs, formerly employed in the fields, were dwindling in number and there was not at hand the usual supply from which their workers were recruited. A large number of these foreigners had been called back to their fatherland to engage in the World War.

In January of 1916, therefore, the tobacco growers of Connecticut met in conference to give this question serious consideration.   Mr. Floyd, the Manager of the Continental Tobacco Corporation, offered a solution for this difficult problem through the further importation of negro labor.   The response to this suggestion was not immediate, because New England had never had large experience with negro labor.   An intense interest in the experiment, however, was aroused through a number of men with connections in the South.   It was decided that the National League on Urban Conditions among Negroes, with headquarters in New York City, should further assist in securing laborers.   Because of the seasonal character of the work, an effort was made to get students from the southern schools by advancing transportation.   The *New York News,* a negro weekly, says of this conference:

Thus was born, right in the heart of Yankee Land, the first significant move to supplant foreign labor with native labor, a step which has resulted in one of the biggest upheavals in the North incident to the European war, which has already been a boon to the colored American, improving his economic status and putting thousands of dollars into his pockets.[1]

The employers of the North felt justified in bringing about a more equitable distribution of the available labor supply in America.   Discussing the labor situation before a conference in New York, Mr. E. J. Traily, Jr., of the Erie Railroad said:

The Erie Railroad has employed a large number of the negro migrants and we are still in need of more because of the abnormal state of labor

[1] *The New York News.*

conditions in this part of the country. It is altogether unfair that the southern States should enforce laws prohibiting the moving of labor from their borders, when there are railroads all over this country that would pay good wages to these laborers. I know of one railroad company last year, which never had a colored man in the service, that was offering large wages and scouring every place for colored help. At the same time the South had and still has a surplus of colored labor and would not permit it to be moved. These conditions actually exist, and I know it. I am interested in this thing not alone from the personal side of it, but due to the fact of my association with the Erie Railroad. I believe that the best thing that this body can do, in my judgment, is to pass resolutions demanding that the United States Emigration Bureau carry out the act passed by Congress empowering the Labor Department to place unoccupied men of other parts of the country where labor is needed.[1]

Early in the summer of 1916, the Pennsylvania and Erie Railroads promiscuously picked up trainloads of negroes from Jacksonville, St. Augustine and Pensacola, Florida. They were at first grouped in camps. The promise of a long free ride to the North met with instant favor, and wild excitement ensued as the news circulated. Carloads of negroes began to pour into Pennsylvania. When they had once touched northern soil and discovered that still higher wages were being offered by other concerns, many deserted the companies responsible for their presence in the North. Some drifted to the steel works of the same State; others left for points nearby. Letters written home brought news of still more enticing fields, and succeeded in stimulating the movement. Of the 12,000 negroes brought into Pennsylvania by the Pennsylvania Railroad, less than 2,000 remained with the company.[2]

It will no doubt be interesting to know exactly where these negroes settled in the North. For the purpose of understanding this distribution the North may well be divided according to the two main lines followed by the migrants in leaving the South. The South and middle Atlantic States sent the majority of their migrants directly up the Atlantic coast while the south central States fed the Northwest. There is, of course, no hard line of separation for these two streams. Laborers were sought

[1] *New York Age*, January 30, 1917; *Christian Recorder*, Philadelphia, February 2, 1917.
[2] *Ibid.*

in fields most accessible to the centers of industry, but individual choice as displayed in the extent of voluntary migration carried them everywhere.

The New England States, which were probably the first to attract this labor, were Connecticut and Massachusetts. The tobacco fields of Connecticut with Hartford as a center received the first negro laborers as mentioned above. Before a year had passed there were over 3,000 southern negroes in the city of Hartford. Massachusetts had its new war plants which served as an attraction. Holyoke received considerable advertisement through the National League on Urban Conditions among Negroes, and as a result secured a number directly from the South. Boston, which has always stood as a symbol of hope for those who sought relief from southern conditions, has not, however, at any time afforded any great variety of occupations for the peasant class of negroes. The receptions staged by the negro leaders of that city were stimulated apparently more by the sentimental causes of the movement than any other consideration. Although there existed in Boston the type of industries which required great numbers of men, barriers prevented negroes in large numbers from entering them and as a result there was no great influx of migrants from the South.

The places mentioned above are, of course, only those which received large numbers. Scattered all over this section of the country were thousands of individuals who, seeking more profitable employment, broke loose from the crowd congregating at favorite points. New York State with New York City as its center has received a considerable number. New York City, however, has been principally a rerouting point. In fact, many of those who subsequently went to New England first went to New York City. The State of New York recruited its labor here. There came to New York probably no less than 75,000 negroes, a large portion of whom stopped in New York City, although Albany, Poughkeepsie, Buffalo and smaller cities received their share.

New Jersey, because of the great number of its industrial plants, was rapidly filled. Newark alone augmented its colored population within a little over a year by one hundred per cent. The attractions in this State were the munitions plants, brick yards and wire factories. The principal cities here that might be mentioned are Newark, Trenton and Jersey City, although the migration to the last two cities hardly compares in volume to that of Newark. Delaware, bordering New Jersey, received a few.[1] Washington, the Capital City and the gateway to the North, already containing the largest negro population of any city in the country was in the path of the migration and had its increase of population accelerated by the war. A considerable number of southern negroes found work there, principally in domestic service. Pennsylvania, the first northern State to begin *wholesale* importation of labor from the South, is the seat of the country's largest steel plants and is the terminal of three of the country's greatest railroad systems. Pittsburgh received perhaps the largest number; Philadelphia and Harrisburg followed in order. The numerous little industrial centers dotting the State fed from the supply furnished by the railroads.[2]

The migration to the Northwest was more extensive. Ohio, the State of vital historical association for negroes, was generously visited. Cleveland, Columbus, Cincinnati, Akron and Youngstown were popular centers. The coal mines, factories and iron works were most in need of men, and obtained them without any great difficulty. Indiana, still probably remembered as the delicate spot in the inquiry following a similar migration thirty-nine years ago, with its very highly developed industries caught the flood proceeding up the Mississippi valley. Indianapolis was a popular point although not a satisfactory one for the migrants, who pretty generally left it for better fields. Gary and Indiana Harbor, more properly satellite cities of Chicago, developed an almost entirely new negro population.

Missouri, a border State, has one city with a considerably augmented negro population. The size of the new population of St. Louis can be accounted for by the fact that geographically it is the first city of the North. East St. Louis, recently made

[1] Fortune, *Report on Negro Migration to the East.*
[2] *Ibid.*

notorious by the reception which it accorded its newcomers, is surrounded by a number of satellite towns, all of which made bids for labor from the South and received it. Not a few negro laborers went to Kansas City from which many were re-routed to other points. Nebraska received a large number of migrants as a direct result of self-advertisement. Omaha was the city which invited them and received the bulk of immigration to that State.

Illinois, the one State known throughout the South because of Chicago, received probably the heaviest quota of any. Located as it is in the center of industry for the Middle West and known to negroes as a " fair " State, it received through Chicago as many at least as the entire State of Pennsylvania. Chicago is the center of a cluster of industrial towns. It has served as a point of distribution through its numerous employment agencies for the territory northwest and northeast. Michigan has one large city, Detroit, which has recently increased its population one hundred per cent because of its number of highly developed industries which have supplied employment for its rapidly increasing population.[1]

The eastern cities which made efforts through various means to augment their labor supply were Pittsburgh, Philadelphia, Newark, New York City and Hartford. It is manifestly impossible to get reliable figures on the volume of increase in the negro population of any of these cities. All that is available is in the form of estimates which can not be too confidently relied upon. Estimates based on the average number of arrivals from the South per day, the increase in the school population and the opinions of social agencies which have engaged themselves in adjusting the newcomers to their new homes appear to agree in the main.

---

[1] These estimates are based upon the reports of investigators sent to make a study of the condition of the migrants.

CHAPTER VI

The Draining of the Black Belt

In order better to understand the migration movement, a special study of it was made for five adjoining States, Georgia, Florida, Alabama, Mississippi and Louisiana, from which came more than half of all migrants. The negro population of these five States was 4,115,299, which was almost half of the negro population of the South. In the particular sections of these States where the migration was the heaviest, the one crop system, cotton, was general. As a result of the cotton price demoralization resulting from the war, the labor depression, the ravages of the cotton boll weevil, and in some regions unusual floods, as already stated, there was in this section of the South an exceptionally large amount of surplus labor. The several trunk line railroads directly connecting this section with the northern industrial centers made the transportation of this labor an easy matter.

In 1915, the labor depression in Georgia was critical and work at remunerative wages was scarce. In Atlanta strong pressure was brought to bear to have the negroes employed in cleaning the streets replaced by whites who were out of work. It was reported that the organized charities of Macon, in dealing with the question of the unemployed, urged whites employing negroes to discharge the blacks and hire whites. Mr. Bridges Smith, the mayor of the city, bitterly opposed this suggestion. When the 1915 cotton crop began to ripen it was proposed to compel the unemployed negroes in the towns to go to the fields and pick cotton. Commenting editorially on this, the *Atlanta Constitution* said:

The problem of the unemployed in Albany, Georgia, is being dealt with practically. All negroes who have not regular employment are offered it in the cotton fields, the immense crop requiring more labor than the plantations ordinarily have. If the unemployed refuse the opportunity, the order "move on" and out of the community is given by the chief of police, and the order must be obeyed. Though the government is taking up very systematically the problem of the unemployed, its solving will be slow, and the government aid for a long time will have to be supplementary to work in this direction, initiated in communities, municipalities and States, where the problem of the unemployed is usually complex.[1]

In the course of time, when the negroes did leave, they departed in such large numbers that their going caused alarm. Because they left at night the number of negroes going north from the immediate vicinity was not generally realized. One night nearly fifty of Tifton boarded northbound passenger trains, which already carried, it is said, some three hundred negroes. Labor agents had been very active in that section all fall, but so cleverly had they done their work that officers had not been able to get a line on them. For several weeks, the daily exodus, it is said, had ranged from ten to twenty-five.[2]

Columbus was an assembling point for migrants going from east Alabama and west Georgia. Railroad tickets would be bought from local stations to Columbus, and there the tickets or transportation for the North, mainly to Chicago, would be secured. Americus was in many respects similarly affected, having had many of its important industries thereby paralyzed. Albany, a railroad center, became another assembling point for migrants from another area. Although difficulties would be experienced in leaving the smaller places directly for the North, it was easy to purchase a ticket to Albany and later depart from that town. The result was that Albany was the point of departure for several thousand negroes, of whom a very large percentage did not come from the towns or Dougherty county in which Albany is situated.[3]

[1] *Atlanta Constitution,* August 28, 1915.
[2] *Ibid.,* December 13, 1916.
[3] A leading colored physician of Albany in commenting on the exodus said: "A considerable number went from town and county. The number was not near so great, however, as from other counties." He was of the opinion that not more than eight or ten families had left. He said that his practice had not been affected. Individuals came in from other sections and took the place of those who went away. He was of the opinion that the fever was about over. This was due to the shortage of labor created by the draft, the increase in wages and better treatment, particularly the

A negro minister, well acquainted with the situation in southwest Georgia, was of the opinion that the greatest number had gone from Thomas and Mitchell counties and the towns of Pelham and Thomasville. Valdosta, with a population of about 8,000 equally divided between the races became a clearing house for many migrants from southern Georgia. The pastor of one of the leading churches said that he lost twenty per cent of his members. The industrial insurance companies reported a twenty per cent loss in membership.[1] Waycross,[2] a railroad center in

latter. Tenants on plantations were receiving better treatment than they formerly received. Some plantation owners as an inducement to their tenants were furnishing each with a cow and a sow. Farm labor which was formerly paid $8 to $12 per month, now received from $20 to $30 per month. He said he knew of one plantation owner who was paying his hands $1.25 per day. This doctor said he was reliably informed that many negroes had left Lee and Calhoun counties and the whites had to go in the fields and plow. As a result of the exodus, the white and colored men of Albany had got closer together. He had recently been elected a member of the Albany Chamber of Commerce, and he understood that about twelve colored men had been invited to become members of the Chamber to assist in working for the development of the county.

One of the colored druggists in Georgia said that Albany was a central point, and that a great many came from Cuthbert, Arlington, Leary and Calhoun, Early and Miller counties to Albany as a starting point for the North. Many went from Albany to Chicago and Philadelphia, but he was of the opinion that the largest number had gone to New Jersey. Migration has been affected by the draft and new opportunities opening up in the South. He said that whites became alarmed and called a meeting and invited some colored persons to consult with them.—Work, *Report on Migration from Georgia.*

[1] " The migration of negroes from this city to the North set in again this week, after a comparative lull of two months. A party of twelve left here yesterday for Jersey City, while twenty others are expected to leave shortly. Many women are going with the men, in some cases leaving their children. Stories of suffering from cold, brought back by negroes during this winter, checked the movement considerably. Several hundred negroes will leave here this spring."—*Atlanta Constitution,* March 26, 1917.

[2] A report from there, in the *Savannah Morning News,* of December 3, 1916, said: " Hundreds of negroes in this section recently have been fleeced by white men posing as agents of large employment bureaus and industrial companies in the eastern States. The most recent instance of the easy marks is reported from Coffee county, but it is in line with what has been happening in other counties. The so-called agent collects a registration fee, giving in return for the money, usually one or two dollars, a card which is said to entitle the bearer to a position at such and such a plant. The negroes get on the train on the date specified, the agent meeting them at the station. He tells them he will have a party ticket for the entire number and to tell the conductor to collect their fares from him. The negroes of course leave home for the point where they think they will be given work, and apparently are a happy lot. But when ticket collecting time comes there is another story to tell.

" Thirty-seven negroes the other day boarded a northbound train at Douglas for Pittsburgh. The agent was on hand to check each one and

the wire grass section of the State, with a population of 7,700 whites and 6,700 negroes, suffered greatly from the migration. Hundreds of negroes in this section were induced by the employment bureaus and industrial companies in eastern States to abandon their homes. From Brunswick, one of the two principal seaports in Georgia, went 1,000 negroes, the chief occupation of whom was stevedoring.   Savannah, another important seaport on the south Atlantic coast, with a population of about 70,000, saw the migration attain unusually large proportions, so as to cause almost a panic and to lead to drastic measures to check it.

The migration was from all sections of Florida. The heaviest movements were from west Florida, from Tampa and Jacksonville. Capitola early reported that a considerable number of negroes left that vicinity, some going north, a few to Jacksonville and others to south Florida to work on the truck farms and in the phosphate mines. A large number of them migrated from Tallahassee to Connecticut to work in the tobacco fields. Owing to the depredations of the boll weevil, many others went north. Most of the migration in west Florida, however, was rural as there are very few large towns in that section. Yet, although they had no such assembling points as there were in other parts of the South, about thirty or thirty-five per cent of the labor left. In north central Florida near Apalachicola fifteen or twenty per cent of the labor left. In middle Florida around Ocala and Gainesville probably twenty to twenty-five per cent of the laborers left, chiefly because of the low wages. The stretch of territory between Pensacola and Jacksonville was said to be one of the most neglected sections in the South, the migration being largely of farm tenants with a considerable number of farm owners. There were cases of the migration of a whole community including the pastor of the church.[1]

then he got aboard, or so the negroes thought. A few miles from Douglas the conductor found he had thirty-seven ticketless passengers. And none of the negroes had the money to pay the fare to Pittsburgh. The train was stopped, and the negroes returned home, wiser and vowing they were 'done with leaving home.' Quite a number of negroes have come to Waycross to meet agents and go north. Before coming here the negroes of course had contributed."

[1] Work, *Report on the Migration from Florida.*

Live Oak, a small town in Sewanee county, experienced the same upheaval, losing a large proportion of its colored population. Dunnelon, a small town in the southern part of Marion county, soon found itself in the same situation. Lakeland, in Polk county, lost about one-third of its negroes. Not less than one-fourth of the black population of Orlando was swept into this movement. Probably half of the negroes of Palatka, Miami and De Land, migrated as indicated by schools and churches, the membership of which decreased one-half. From 3,000 to 5,000 negroes migrated from Tampa and Hillsboro county. Jacksonville, the largest city in Florida, with a population of about 35,000 negroes, lost about 6,000 or 8,000 of its own black population and served as an assembling point for 14,000 or 15,000 others who went to the North.[1]

By September, 1916, the movement in Alabama was well under way. In Selma there was made the complaint that a new scheme was being used to entice negroes away. Instead of advertising in Alabama papers, the schemes of the labor agents were proclaimed through papers published in other States and circulated in Alabama. As a result there was a steady migration of negroes from Alabama to the North and to points in Tennessee and Arkansas where conditions were more inviting and wages higher. Estimates appear to indicate, however, that Alabama, through the migration, lost a larger proportion of her negro population than did any one of the other southern States.[2]

From Eufaula in the eastern part of the State it was reported in September that trains leaving there on Sundays in 1916 were packed with negroes going north, that hundreds left, joining crowds from Clayton, Clio and Ozark. There seemed to be a " free ride " every Sunday and many were giving up lucrative positions there to go. The majority of these negroes, however, went from the country where they had had a disastrous experience with the crops of the year 1916 on account of the July floods.[3] By October the exodus from Dallas county

[1] Work, *Report on the Migration from Florida.*
[2] Work, *Report on the Migration from Alabama.*
[3] *Montgomery (Alabama) Advertiser,* September 27, 1916.

had reached such alarming proportions that farmers and business men were devising means to stop it.

Bullock county, with a working population of 15,000 negroes, lost about one-third and in addition about 1,500 non-workers. The reports of churches as to the loss of membership at certain points justify this conclusion. Hardly any of the churches escaped without a serious loss and the percentage in most cases was from twenty-five to seventy per cent.[1] It seemed that these intolerable conditions did not obtain in Union Springs. According to persons living in Kingston, the wealthiest and the most prosperous negroes of the district migrated. In October, 1916, some of the first large groups left Mobile, Alabama, for the Northwest. The report says: " Two trainloads of negroes were sent over the Louisville and Nashville Railroad to work in the railroad yards and on the tracks in the West. Thousands more are expected to leave during the next month."

As soon as the exodus got well under way, Birmingham became one of the chief assembling points in the South for the migrants and was one of the chief stations on the way north. Thousands came from the flood and boll weevil districts to Birmingham. The records of the negro industrial insurance companies showed the effects of the migration both from and to Birmingham. The Atlanta Mutual Insurance Company lost 500 of its members and added 2,000. Its debit for November, 1916, was $502.25; for November, 1917, it was $740. The business of the Union Central Relief Association was greatly affected by the migration. The company in 1916 lost heavily. In 1917 it cleared some money.

The State of Mississippi, with a larger percentage of negroes than any other State in the Union, naturally lost a large number of its working population. There has been in progress

---

[1] The investigator had been in Union Springs on a Saturday before there was a migration. The crowds on the streets were so great that it was difficult for one to pass. On Saturday, November 17, 1917, the investigator was again in Union Springs. It was an ideal autumn day. Good crops had been made in the county. Especially high prices were being paid for all sorts of farm produce. The market season was on. Court was in session. The streets, however, had about the crowds to be found on some days, other than Saturday, before the migration began.

for a number of years a movement from the hill counties of the State of Mississippi to the Delta, and from the Delta to Arkansas. The interstate migration has resulted from the land poverty of the hill country and from intimidation of the " poor whites " particularly in Amite, Lincoln, Franklin and Wilkinson counties. In 1908 when the floods and boll weevil worked such general havoc in the southwestern corner of the State, labor agents from the Delta went down and carried away thousands of families. It is estimated that more than 8,000 negroes left Adams county during the first two years of the boll weevil period. Census figures for 1910 show that the southwestern counties suffered a loss of 18,000 negroes. The migration of recent years to adjacent States has been principally to Arkansas.[1]

Jackson, the capital of Mississippi, seriously felt the migration. The majority of the " lower middle class " of negroes, twenty-five per cent of the business men and fully one-third of the professional men left the city—in all between 2,000 and 5,000. Two of the largest churches lost their pastors and about 200 of each of their memberships. Other churches suffered a decrease of forty per cent in their communicants. Two-thirds of the remaining families in Jackson are part families with relatives who have recently migrated to the North.

For years the negroes of Greenville have been unsettled and dissatisfied to the extent of leaving. Negroes came from Leland to Greenville to start for the North. This condition has obtained there ever since the World's Fair in Chicago, when families first learned to go to that section whenever opportunities for establishment were offered them. Although the negroes from Greenville are usually prosperous, during this exodus they have mortgaged their property or placed it in the hands of friends on leaving for the North. Statistics indicate

---

[1] The reasons back of this, as obtained from migrants themselves, are that, except in the town of Mound Bayou, negroes have not been encouraged to own property or rent, but to work on shares; in Arkansas it is possible to buy good land cheaply and on reasonable terms; inducements are offered by Arkansas in the form of better treatment and schools; there are no such " excessive " taxes as are required in the Mississippi Delta to protect them from the overflows; the boll weevil has not yet seriously affected that State, and a small farmer may be fairly independent in Arkansas.

that in the early part of the movement at least 1,000 left the immediate vicinity of Greenville and since that time others have continued to go in large numbers.[1]

Greenwood, with a population evenly balanced between the white and black, had passed through the unusual crisis of bad crops and the invasion of the boll weevil. The migration from this point, therefore, was at first a relief to the city rather than a loss. The negroes, in the beginning, therefore, moved into the Delta and out to Arkansas until the call for laborers in the North. The migration from this point to the North reached its height in the winter and spring of 1916 and 1917. The migrants would say that they were going to Memphis, but when you next heard from them they would be in Chicago, St. Louis or Detroit. The police at the Illinois Central depot had been handling men roughly. When they were rude to one, ten or twelve left. Young men usually left on night trains. Next day their friends would say, "Ten left last night," or, " Twelve left last night." In this manner the stream started. Friends would notify others of the time and place of special trains. The type of negro leaving is indicated in the decline in the church membership. Over 300 of those who left were actively connected with some church. During the summer of 1917, 100 houses

---

[1] The lumber mills and the local corporations provide a great part of the work for laborers in the city. Wages last year ranged from $1.25 to $1.50 a day. Wages at present are $1.75 and $2 a day. Cotton picking last year brought 60 and 75 cents a hundred; at present $2 is paid for every hundred pounds picked. The city has enacted " move on " laws intending to get rid of drones. The police, it is said, could not distinguish drones from " all negroes."

It was further complained that the police deputies and sheriffs are too free with the use of their clubs and guns when a negro is involved. It was related that Dr. ——, practising 47 years in Greenville, Mississippi, was driving his buggy in a crowded street on circus day when he was commanded by a policeman to drive to one side and let a man pass. He replied that he could not because he himself was jammed. He was commanded again and then dragged from the buggy, clubbed and haled into the police court and fined. The officer who arrested him swore that he had given frequent trouble. which was untrue according to reliable testimony and his own statement. This incident is also told:

A policeman's friend needed a cook. The policeman drove by a negro home and, seeing a woman on the porch, told her to get in the buggy. No questions were permitted. She was carried to his friend's home and told to work., The woman prepared one meal and left the city for the North.— Johnson, *Report on the Migration from Mississippi*.

stood vacant in the town and over 300 were abandoned in the McShein addition. As the crops were gathered people moved in from the country, from the southern part of the State and from the "hills" generally to take the places of those who had left for the North.

There was no concerted movement from Clarksdale, a town with a population of about 400 whites and 600 blacks; but families appeared to slip away because of the restlessness and uneasiness in evidence everywhere. From the rural district around there was considerable migration to Arkansas, but considerable numbers were influenced to leave for Buffalo and Chicago. Mound Bayou lost some of its population also to Arkansas and the North, as they could buy land cheaper in the former and find more lucrative employment in the latter. Natchez did not suffer a serious loss of population until the invasion of the boll weevil and the floods.

Hattiesburg, a large lumber center, was at the beginning of the exodus, almost depopulated. Some of the first migrants went to Pennsylvania but the larger number went to Chicago. It became a rallying point for many negroes who assembled there ostensibly to go to New Orleans, at which place they easily provided for their transportation to Chicago and other points in the North. From Laurel in Jones county, a large sawmill district, it is estimated that between 4,000 and 5,000 negroes moved north. About 3,000 left Meridian for Chicago, St. Louis, Detroit and Pittsburgh. Indianola, a town with a number of negro independent enterprises, also became upset by this movement, losing a considerable number of progressive families. Gulfport, a coast town a short distance from New Orleans, lost about one-third of its negro population. About 45 families left Bobo for Arkansas, and 15 families went to the North. Johnstown, Mississippi, lost 150 of its 400 negroes.[1]

The owners of turpentine industries and lumber plants in southeastern Mississippi were especially affected by the exodus. In Hinds, Copiah, Lincoln, Rankin, Newton and Lake counties, many white residents rather than suffer their crops to be lost,

[1] Johnson, *Report on the Migration from Mississippi.*

worked in the fields. It was reported that numbers of these whites were leaving for the Delta and for Kentucky, Tennessee and Arkansas. Firms there attempted to look in the North that they might send for the negroes whom they had previously employed, promising them an advance in wages.

At the same time the Illinois Central Railroad was carrying from New Orleans and other parts of Louisiana thousands into Indiana, Illinois and Michigan. At the Illinois Central Railroad station in that city, the agent had been having his hands full taking names of colored laborers wanting and waiting to go North. About the first of April, 1917, there came also the reports from New Orleans that 300 negro laborers left there on the Southern Pacific steamer for New York, and 500 more left later on another of the same company's steamships bound also for New York, it was said, to work for the company. Thousands thus left for the North and West and East, the number reaching over 1,200.

It is an interesting fact that this migration from the South followed the path marked out by the Underground Railroad of antebellum days. Negroes from the rural districts moved first to the nearest village or town, then to the city. On the plantations it was not regarded safe to arrange for transportation to the North through receiving and sending letters. On the other hand, in the towns and cities there was more security in meeting labor agents. The result of it was that cities like New Orleans, Birmingham, Jacksonville, Savannah and Memphis became concentration points. From these cities migrants were rerouted along the lines most in favor.

The principal difference between this course and the Underground Railroad was that in the later movement the southernmost States contributed the largest numbers. This perhaps is due in part to the selection of Florida and Georgia by the first concerns offering the inducement of free transportation, and at the same time it accounts for the very general and intimate knowledge of the movement by the people in States through which they were forced to pass. In Hattiesburg, Mississippi, for example, the first intimation of a great movement of negroes to the North came through reports that thousands of negroes were leaving Florida for the North. To the negroes of Florida, South Carolina, Virginia and Georgia the North means Pennsylvania, New Jersey, New York and New England. The route is more direct, and it is this section of the northern expanse of the United States that gets widest advertisement through tourists, and passengers and porters on the Atlantic coast steamers. The northern newspapers with the greatest circulation are from Pennsylvania and New York, and the New York colored weeklies are widely read. Reports from all of these south Atlantic States indicate that comparatively few persons ventured into the Northwest when a better known country lay before them.

The Pennsylvania Railroad, one of the first to import laborers in large numbers, reports that of the 12,000 persons brought to Pennsylvania over its road, all but 2,000 were from Florida and Georgia. The tendency was to continue along the first definite path. Each member of the vanguard controlled a small group of friends at home, if only the members of his immediate family. Letters sent back, representing that section of the North and giving directions concerning the route best known, easily influenced the next groups to join their friends rather than explore new fields. In fact, it is evident throughout the movement that the most congested points in the North when the migration reached its height, were those favorite cities to which the first group had gone.[1] An intensive study of a group of 77 families from the South, selected at random in Chicago, showed but one family from Florida and no representation at all from North and South Carolina. A tabulation of figures and facts from 500 applications for work by the Chicago League on Urban Conditions among Negroes gives but a few persons from North Carolina, twelve from South Carolina and one from Virginia. The largest number, 102, came from Georgia. Applicants for work in New York from the south Atlantic States are overwhelming.[2]

[1] Johnson, *Report on the Migration from Mississippi.*
[2] *Ibid.*

For the east and west south central States, the Northwest was more accessible and better known. St. Louis and Cincinnati are the nearest northern cities to the South and excursions have frequently been run there from New Orleans, through the State of Mississippi. There are in St. Louis, as in other more northern cities, little communities of negroes from the different sections of the South. The mail order and clothing houses of Chicago have advertised this city throughout the South. The convenience of transportation makes the Northwest a popular destination for migrants from Mississippi, Alabama, Louisiana, Texas and Tennessee. The Illinois Central Railroad runs directly to New Orleans through Tennessee and Mississippi.

There were other incidental factors which determined the course of the movement. Free trains from different sections broke new paths by overcoming the obstacles of funds for transportation. No questions were asked of the passengers, and, in some instances, as many as were disposed to leave were carried. When once they had advanced beyond the Mason and Dixon line, many fearing that fees for transportation would be deducted from subsequent pay, if they were in the employ of the parties who, as they understood, were advancing their fares, deserted the train at almost any point that looked attractive. Employment could be easily secured and at good wages. Many of these unexpected and premature destinations became the nucleuses for small colonies whose growth was stimulated and assisted by the United States postal service.

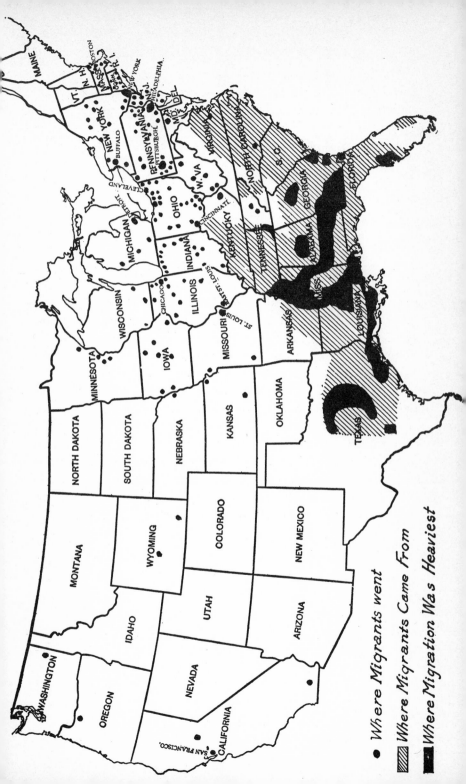

Where Migrants went

Where Migrants Came From

Where Migration Was Heaviest

CHAPTER VII

Efforts to Check the Movement

The departure of the first negroes usually elicited no concern from the authorities. It was assumed that their actions were merely expressions of the negro's "love for travel," and that they would soon return. When, however, they did not return and hosts of others followed, the white South became deeply concerned and endeavored to check the movement. Throughout the exodus drastic legislation and force were employed. In Alabama, Arkansas, Mississippi and Georgia laws were passed in an effort to suppress the activities of labor agents. Licenses were made prohibitively high; labor agents were arrested and heavily fined. In some cases their coming was penalized to prohibit their operations entirely and they frequently suffered physical injury.

In Florida labor recruiting early assumed a serious aspect. Precaution was, therefore, taken to impede the progress of the work of labor agents among negroes, at first by moral suasion and then by actual force. The cities and towns of this State enacted measures requiring a very high license of labor agents, imposing in case of failure to comply with these regulations, a penalty of imprisonment. For example, in Tampa when these operations were brought to the attention of the authorities, Joe Robinson, a negro officer, was detailed to investigate the matter. He discovered that one Joyce and another negro named Alex Reeves were implicated in the movement. These men were charged with having collected $7 from each of several hundred negroes who wanted to go to Pennsylvania. A meeting among the negroes of Tampa was then held to secure pledges of assistance for the negro officer, then making an effort to prevent the exodus. Being under the impression that the ignorant members of their race were being imposed upon by agents from without, many of these leading negroes pledged themselves to assist in the suppression of it.[1]

In Jacksonville, where the labor agents flourished, the City Council passed an ordinance requiring that migration agents should pay $1,000 license to recruit labor sent out of the State under penalty of $600 fine and 60 days in jail. Several police detectives were assigned the task of arresting those who were said to be spreading false reports among negroes there to the effect that special trains were ready on various specified dates to take them to points in the North. When, therefore, large crowds of negroes gathered near the Union Depot in Jacksonville, awaiting the so-called special train, they were handled rather roughly by the police when it was shown that they had not purchased tickets and there was no one to vouch for their transportation.

The same condition with respect to the apparent necessity for prohibitive measures obtained in Georgia. The local governments early took action to prevent the drain of the labor population to northern States through the operation of labor agents. It was soon observed, however, that these agents worked out their schemes so clandestinely that it was impossible to check the movement by such measures. Fearing that the general unrest among the negroes of the city and the efforts that were being put forth on the part of the authorities to keep them from being transported from Macon to the North, might result in a riot with which the city authorities would not be able to cope, Chief of Police George S. Riley recommended to the civil service commission that forty magazine rifles be purchased for the police department.[2] At that time the police had only their pistols and clubs. It was said that surliness then existed among certain negroes and the police wanted to be able to cope with any situation that might arise. The City Council, thereafter, raised the license fee for labor agents to $25,000, requiring also that such an agent be recommended by ten local ministers, ten manufacturers and twenty-five business men. The

---

[1] Work, *Report on the Migration from Florida.*
[2] *Atlantic Constitution,* November 1, 1916.

police of Macon were very active in running down labor agents violating this law.

Americus was honeycombed and carefully watched and searched for persons inducing negroes to migrate, as there was a large exodus of negroes from this city to the tobacco fields of Connecticut. Negroes attempting to leave were arrested and held to see if by legal measures they could be deterred from going North. The officers in charge of this raid were armed with State warrants charging misdemeanors and assisted by a formidable array of policemen and deputy sheriffs. Negroes were roughly taken from the trains and crowded into the prisons to await trial for these so-called misdemeanors. Although the majority of them were set free after their trains had left the city, the leaders in most cases suffered humiliation at the hands of the officers of the law.[1]

At Thomasville, a white man and a negro were arrested, charged with the usual crime of being labor agents. Much excitement followed. Fearing serious results, the colored ministers of this city endeavored to stop the exodus. A committee of their most prominent citizens met with the mayor and discussed the matter freely. They arranged for a large mass meeting of white and colored citizens who undertook to cooperate in bringing the exodus to an end. The white citizens of Waycross experienced the same trouble with labor agents, but had much difficulty in finding out exactly who they were and how they contrived to make such inroads on the population.[2]

The situation became more critical in Savannah, one of the largest assembling points for migrants in the South. When the loss of labor became so serious and ordinary efforts to check it failed, more drastic measures were resorted to. On the thirteenth of August, for example, when there spread through the city the rumor that two special trains would leave for the North there followed great commotion among the negroes, who, already much disturbed by the agitation for and against the movement, were easily induced to start for the North. When, at about five

[1] Work, *Report on the Migration from Georgia.*
[2] *Ibid.*

o'clock that morning, 2,000 negroes assembled at the station for this purpose, the county police, augmented by a detachment of city officers, appeared at the station and attempted to clear the tracks; but the crowd being so large the officers finally found their task impossible, for as they would clear one section of the tracks the crowd would surge to another. The crowd was extremely orderly and good natured and the two arrests that were made were for minor offenses. As these trains failed to move according to orders, over 300 of this group paid their own fares and proceeded to the North.[1]

A few days later Savannah reached a crisis in the labor movement agitation, when over 100 negroes were placed under arrest at the Union Depot and sent to the police barracks. Several patrol wagon loads of police arrived at the station and immediately a cordon was formed by the police around all negroes in the lobby and every exit from the station was guarded. By this unusual sight many persons were attracted to the station and excitement ran high. Many negroes were arrested with a view to finding out the leaders of the movement, but upon failure to discover the facts in the case the lieutenant in charge ordered the men in custody to be incarcerated on charges of loitering.

To show how groundless these charges were, one need but to note the character of some of the persons arrested. Four carpenters from Lumpkin, Georgia, had just arrived and were waiting for a contractor for whom they had agreed to work a short distance from the city. Another young man entered the station to purchase a ticket to Burroughs, Georgia, to see relatives, but he was not only incarcerated but had to give a bond of $100 for his appearance next morning. Another young man, working for the Pullman Company, entered the depot to cash a check for $11 when he was arrested, sent to jail and searched. Still another, a middle-aged man of most pleasing appearance, had just arrived from Jacksonville, Florida, and was waiting in the station until the time to proceed by boat that afternoon to New York. On one occasion, J. H. Butler, manager of the

---

[1] Work, *Report on the Migration from Georgia.*

Savannah Tribune, a negro newspaper, was arrested charged with violation of the city and State law of sending labor out of the city. He was obliged to give bond of $400 to appear in court the next day. At the same time seventeen college boys who were waiting at a New York steamer dock were also apprehended. The trial of the men before the recorder proved farcical, not a single one of the hundred or more prisoners being required to testify. After the chief of the detective force and several police lieutenants had testified, Recorder Schwartz ordered the men all released, but not before he had taken occasion to upbraid the police force for the unnecessarily large number of arrests.[1]

Alabama was equally alive to the need to suppress the migration propaganda among negroes. To this end the Montgomery City Commission on September 19, 1916, passed an ordinance to the effect that any person who would entice, persuade or influence any laborer or other person to leave the city of Montgomery for the purpose of being employed at any other place as a laborer must on conviction be fined not less than one nor more than one hundred dollars, or may be sentenced to hard labor for the city, for not more than six months, one or both in the discretion of the court. The other ordinance provided that any person, firm or corporation who published, printed or wrote or delivered or distributed or posted or caused to be published, printed or written or delivered or distributed or posted, any advertisement, letter, newspaper, pamphlet, handbill or other writing, for the purpose of enticing, persuading or influencing any laborer or other person to leave the city of Montgomery for the purpose of being employed at any other place as a laborer must on conviction be fined not less than one hundred dollars, or may be sentenced to hard labor for the city for not more than six months, one or both in the discretion of the court. Labor agents and other leaders both white and black were arrested throughout the State in accordance with the usual custom of preferring technical charges.[2]

The treatment of the movement in Mississippi was no ex-

[1] Work, *Report on the Migration from Georgia.*
[2] Work, *Report on the Migration from Alabama.*

ception to the rule. At Jackson, the "pass riders," as they were called, were so molested by the police that they were finally driven from the town. In the same town the citizens were reported to have forced the railroads to discontinue the use of passes on the threat of damaging their interests and influencing decisions in court cases. Negroes were secretly enticed away, however, after they had been dispersed from the railway stations and imprisoned when in the act of boarding the trains. The police interfered at one time with negroes leaving, especially when it was suspected that they were leaving on passes. To circumvent this, negroes would go two or three stations below Jackson where there were no policemen and board the trains. It was the unanimous opinion of whites and blacks who observed the almost frantic efforts to leave the town, that any attempt to hinder by intimidation or by making it difficult to leave, simply served to make them more determined to leave.[1]

At Greenville, Mississippi, trains were stopped. Negroes were dragged therefrom and others were prevented from boarding them. Strangers were searched for evidence that might convict them as labor agents. It is also reported that local authorities were reprimanded for interfering with interstate commerce. At Greenwood there was much complaint against the brutality of the police, whose efforts to intimidate negroes carried them beyond bounds. A chartered car carrying fifty men and women was sidetracked at Brookhaven for three days. The man conducting the passengers was arrested, but when no charge was brought against him, he was released.[2]

A Hattiesburg, Mississippi, ticket agent attempted on the advice of citizens to interfere with negroes leaving by refusing to sell tickets. Some one called the attention of the general superintendent to the matter. Thereafter the man was courteous and even assisted the migrants. Police arrested one or two men at the station, and, according to one of the men, made the crowd so angry that they swore they would not stop until all had gone. There are cited further instances of letters to plan-

---

[1] Johnson, *Report on the Migration from Mississippi.*
[2] *Ibid.*

tation hands which were detained and telegrams which were delayed. At Meridian, Mississippi, a trainload of negroes en route to the North was held up by the chief of police on a technical charge. It is said that the United States marshal arrested him and placed him under heavy bond for delaying the train. The federal authorities were importuned to stop the movement. They withdrew the assistance of the Employment Department, but admitted that they could not stop the interstate migration.[1]

One remarked, however, " It will scarcely be possible, to make a sectional issue of these Columbus convictions, as the charge of ' enticing away of labor ' in that country is aimed at certain Arkansas planters who carried away several carloads of negroes to work on their places, leaving the Mississippi employers without the labor to gather or grow their crops. It can not, therefore, be interpreted as an attempt to keep the negro in semi-slavery in the South and prevent him from going to work at better wages in the northern munition factories; it is only an effort to protect Mississippi employers from Arkansas planters." [2]

The alarm felt over the exodus prompted the mayor of New Orleans to telegraph the president of the Illinois Central Railroad, asking that his road stop carrying negroes to the North. The latter replied that he had viewed with much concern the heavy exodus of negro labor from the South during the past year, and, because of his very important interest in that section, it was not to his advantage to encourage it, but as common carriers, they could not refuse to sell tickets or to provide the necessary transportation. It seemed to him that as long as their friends and kinsmen who had preceded them to the North and East were receiving a high scale of wages, the South would have to look for continued movement.[3]

After having enforced these drastic measures without securing satisfactory results, and having seen that any attempt to hold the negroes by force resulted apparently in an increased determination to leave, there was resort to the policy of frightening

[1] Johnson, *Report on the Migration from Mississippi.*
[2] *Times Picayune,* New Orleans, October 1, 1916.
[3] Work, *Report on the Migration from Louisiana.*

the negroes away from the North by circulating rumors as to the misfortunes to be experienced there. Negroes were then warned against the rigors of the northern winter and the death rate from pneumonia and tuberculosis. Social workers in the North reported frequent cases of men with simple colds who actually believed that they had developed " consumption." Speakers who wished to discourage the exodus reported " exact " figures on the death rate of the migrants in the North that were astounding. As, for example, it was said by one Reverend Mr. Parks that there were 2,000 of· them sick in Philadelphia. The editor of a leading white paper in Jackson, Mississippi, made the remark that he feared that the result of the first winter's experience in the North would prove serious to the South, in so far as it would remove the bugbear of the northern climate. The returned migrants were encouraged to speak in disparagement of the North and to give wide publicity to their utterances, emphasizing incidents of suffering reported through the press.

When such efforts as these failed, however, the disconcerted planters and business men of the South resorted to another plan. Reconciliation and persuasion were tried. Meetings were held and speakers were secured and advised what to say. In cities and communities where contact on this plane had been infrequent, it was a bit difficult to approach the subject. The press of Georgia gave much space to the discussion of the movement and what ought to be done to stop it. The consensus of opinion of the white papers in the State was that the negro had not been fairly treated, and that better treatment would be one of the most effective means of checking the migration. Mob violence, it was pointed out, was one of the chief causes of the exodus.[1]

The *Tifton* (Georgia) *Gazette* commenting on the causes said:

They have allowed negroes to be lynched, five at a time, on nothing stronger than suspicion; they have allowed whole sections to be depopulated of them (notably in several north Georgia counties); they have allowed

[1] Johnson, *Report on the Migration from Mississippi.*

them to be whitecapped and to be whipped, and their homes burned, with
only the weakest and most spasmodic efforts to apprehend or punish those
guilty—when any efforts were made at all. Loss of much of the State's
best labor is one of the prices Georgia is paying for unchecked mob activity
against negroes often charged only with ordinary crimes. Current dispatches from Albany, Georgia, in the center of the section apparently most
affected, and where efforts are being made to stop the exodus by spreading
correct information among the negroes, say that the heaviest migration of
negroes has been from those counties in which there have been the worst
outbreaks against negroes. It is developed by investigation that where there
have been lynchings, the negroes have been most eager to believe what the
emigration agents have told them of plots for the removal or extermination
of the race. Comparatively few negroes have left Dougherty county, which
is considered significant in view of the fact that this is one of the counties
in southwest Georgia in which a lynching has never occurred.

At Thomasville, Georgia, a mass meeting of colored citizens
of the town with many from the country was held at the court
house and addresses were made by several prominent white
men, as well as by several colored with a view to taking some
steps in regard to the exodus of negroes from this section to
the North and West. The whole sentiment of the meeting was
very amicable, the negroes applauding enthusiastically the
speeches of the white men and the advice given by them. Resolutions were drawn up by a committee expressing the desire
that the people of the two races continue to live together as
they have done in the past and that steps be taken to adjust any
difference between them.[1]

After a conference of three days at Waycross, Georgia, the
negroes came to a decision as to the best manner in which to
present their cause to the white people with a view to securing
their cooperation towards the improvement of conditions in
the South to make that section more habitable. " There are
four things of which our people complain," they said, " and
this conference urges our white friends to secure for us these
things with all possible speed. First, more protection at the
hands of the law. We ask that the law of the State, made
and enforced by white men, should be made to apply with exact
justice to both races. We have no sympathy for criminals,
but we ask that the innocent shall be protected to the fullest

[1] *Atlanta Constitution,* June 1, 1917.

extent of the law.   Second, that more liberal provisions be made for the education of our people."   They commended Governor Dorsey for his courageous recommendation in his inaugural address that an agricultural school should be established for negroes in some center in southern Georgia, and asked their friends everywhere to urge the members of the legislature from the various counties to put Governor Dorsey's noble sentiments into law.   These memorialists felt, too, that as far as possible, wages should be in keeping with the cost of living, and that the white people generally should take an interest in the general welfare of the negroes.[1]

Tuskegee Institute was also quick to offer a remedy for the migration.   In the latter part of September, 1916, the institution made a strong effort to persuade the negro farmers to remain on the land instead of going to the cities.   Conferences were held with the bankers of Tuskegee and with many planters of Macon county and a method of dealing with the situation was worked out.   This method embraced a number of helpful suggestions as to how to solve their many perplexing problems.[2]

[1] I. D. Davis served as president of the conference and J. B. Ellis as secretary.   Former Superior Court Judge T. A. Parker and V. L. Stanton, president of the Chamber of Commerce, were among the prominent white people who attended.   It was the sense of the conference that the colored people as a race should do all in their power in the present crisis to assist the government and, above all else, to help themselves by conserving food. The president of the conference said the colored people had to work harder than ever before with so many problems confronting their country.   "It is no time for loafing," he said, "we must work early and late, and make our work count.'—*Savannah Morning News,* July 18, 1917.

[2] The suggestions were: to encourage the farmer to plant peanuts, soy beans, velvet beans and cotton as cash crops; to create a cash market for such crops named above as at present have no cash market; to encourage tenants to grow fall and winter gardens and to plant at least five acres of oats to the plow, seed being furnished when necessary; to stipulate, in making tenant contracts for another year, that cotton stalks be plowed under in the fall, that special methods of combating the boll weevil be used. To advance no more than $25 to the plow, and, in every case possible, to refrain from any advance; to encourage land holders to rent land for part of the crops grown; to urge the exercise of leniency on unpaid notes and mortgages due from thrifty and industrious farmers so as to give them a chance to recover from the boll weevil conditions and storm losses; to create a market lasting all year for such crops as hay, cow-peas, sweet potatoes, poultry and live stock; to urge everybody to build fences and make pastures so as to grow more live stock and to produce more nearly all of the supplies used on the farm; to carry on a food campaign in the country, devoting the first Sunday in October to the work of urging the people to plant gardens and sow oats, and to organize a Farmers' Loan Association in Macon

At the twenty-sixth annual negro conference at Tuskegee Institute, the institution took that occasion to send through certain declarations a message to the negroes of the South. These declarations recited the distress and suffering impelling the negroes to migrate, expressing the appreciation of the necessity to do something to better their condition by embracing the new opportunities offered them in the North. On the other hand, this institution felt that there were many permanent opportunities for the masses of the colored people in the South, which is now entering upon a great era of development. Among these are the millions of acres of land yet to be cultivated, cities to be built, railroads to be extended and mines to be worked. These memorialists considered it of still greater importance to the negro that in the South they have acquired land, buildings, etc., valued at about five hundred million dollars. The negroes were, therefore, urged to stay on the soil which they owned.

Addressing a word to the white people of the South, the conference said that the disposition of so many of the blacks to leave is not because they do not love the Southland but because they believe that in the North they will not only have more opportunity to get more money but that they will get better treatment, better protection under the law and better school facilities for their children. The conference urged, therefore, that the southern white people avail themselves of their greatest opportunity to cooperate with the blacks in the various communities and have a thorough understanding as to working for the common welfare of all. The delegates believed that the time had come for the best element of the whites and blacks to unite to protect the interests of both races to the end that more effective work may be done in the upbuilding of a greater South.[1]

In the same way the people of Mississippi soon discovered that any attempt forcibly to hold negroes resulted apparently in an increased determination to leave. Nor was it sufficient

county to work with the Farmers' Loan Bank being established by the United States Government.
[1] Report of the Twenty-sixth Annual Negro Conference at Tuskegee Institute.

to warn the negroes against the rigors of the northern winter and the death rate from pneumonia and tuberculosis. In Greenwood, Mississippi, the difficulty was circumvented by using the Red Cross and the food conservation meetings as a forum for the discussion of the movement. This was the first time that the negroes and whites of Greenwood had met to discuss matters of mutual welfare. Bishop W. P. Thirkield of New Orleans addressed a body of negroes and whites on the movement. He suggested that whites get representative colored persons together and find the cause. He also suggested a remedy through better treatment, more wages and more cooperation between the races. Negro ministers stated that they were offered sums of money by bankers, planters and merchants to speak in discouragement of the movement. Some spoke, and others, by far the greater number, seem to have remained neutral.[1]

It was found necessary to increase wages from ten to twenty-five per cent and in some cases as much as 100 per cent to hold labor. The reasons for migration given by negroes were sought. In almost all cases the chief complaint was about treatment. An effort was made to meet this by calling conferences and by giving publicity to the launching of a campaign to make unfair settlements and other such grievances unpopular. Thus, in Bolivar county, Mississippi, a meeting was called, ostensibly to look after the economic welfare of the Delta country, but in reality to develop some plan for holding labor. A subcommittee of seventeen men was appointed to look into the labor situation. There were twelve white men and five negroes. The subcommittee met and reported to the body that the present labor shortage was due to the migration, and that the migration was due to a feeling of insecurity before the law, the unrestrained action of mobs, unfair methods of yearly settlement on farms and inadequate school facilities. As a result of the report, it was agreed to make an appropriation of $25,000 towards an agricultural high school, as a step towards showing an interest in the negroes of Bolivar county and thus give them reasons for remaining. A campaign was started to make unpopular

[1] Johnson, *Report on the Migration from Mississippi.*

the practice among farmers of robbing negroes of the returns from their labor, and a general effort was made by a few of the leading men behind the movement to create " a better feeling " between the races.[1]

Wide publicity was given to the experiment in plantation government, and the policy was accepted by a number of planters as opportunistic action. Thus, one Mr. Abbott of Natchez, Mississippi, told the planters of his section that good treatment, adequate and sympathetic oversight are the important factors in any effort to hold labor. He made a trip to his farm every week, endeavoring to educate his tenants in modes of right living. Every man on his place had a bank account and was apparently satisfied. This example was presented with the statement that where these methods had been used, few had left. One planter purchased twenty-eight Ford automobiles to sell on easy terms to his tenants with the hope of contenting them.

The newspapers published numerous letters from southern negro leaders urging negroes to consider well their step, asserting that the South is the best place for them and that the southern white man knows them and will in consequence be more lenient with their shortcomings. The papers further urged an increase in wages and better treatment. Wherever possible, there were published articles which pointed to the material prosperity of negroes in the South. For example, a writer of Greenville, said of negroes' loyalty in 1917:

The prosperity as well as the patriotism of the negro farmer has been shown in the purchase of Liberty Bonds in the Delta. Many colored farm laborers subscribed for bonds. Every family on the place of Planter C. D. Walcott, near Hollandale, took a bond, while one negro, Boley Cox, a renter, bought bonds to the amount of $1,000 and gave his check for the total amount out of the savings of this year from his crop and still has cotton to sell. There are negro families on Delta plantations making more money this year than the salary of the governor of the State.

When migrants could be induced to talk freely, they complained also against the treatment in the courts. Some of the cities consequently are known to have suspended their raids

[1] Johnson, *Report on the Migration from Mississippi.*

and arrests on petty charges.   In some instances the attempts
at pacification reached almost incredible bounds.   For example,
a negro missed connection with his train through the fault
of the railroad.   His white friend advised him to bring suit.
This he did and urged as his principal grievance that he was
stranded in a strange town and was forced to sleep in quarters
wholly at the mercy of bed bugs.   It is said that he was awarded
damages to the extent of $800.   A Jackson, Mississippi, daily
paper that had been running a column of humorous incidents
about negroes taken from the daily court sessions, which was
very distasteful to the colored people of the city, discontinued
it.   Such methods as these have been the only ones to prove
effective in bringing about an appreciable stem in the tide.
With the advent of the United States Government constructing
cantonments and establishing manufacturing plants in the South,
the millions thus diverted to that section have caused such an
increase in wages that the movement has been decidedly checked.

CHAPTER VIII

Effects of the Movement on the South

The first changes wrought by this migration were unusually startling. Homes found themselves without servants, factories could not operate because of the lack of labor, farmers were unable to secure laborers to harvest their crops. Streets in towns and cities once crowded assumed the aspect of deserted thoroughfares, houses in congested districts became empty, churches, lodges and societies suffered such a large loss of membership that they had to close up or undergo reorganization.

Probably the most striking change was the unusual increase in wages. The wages for common labor in Thomasville, Georgia, increased almost certainly 100 per cent. In Valdosta there was a general increase in the town and county of about 50 per cent, in Brunswick and Savannah the same condition obtained. The common laborer who had formerly received 80 cents a day earned thereafter $1.50 to $1.75. Farm hands working for from $10 to $15 per month were advanced to $20 or $35 per month. Brick masons who had received 50 cents per hour thereafter earned 62½ cents and 70 cents per hour. In Savannah common laborers paid as high as $2 per day were advanced to $3. At the sugar refinery the rates were for women, 15 to 22 cents per hour, men, 22 to 30 cents per hour. In the more skilled lines of work, the wages were for carpenters, $4 to $6 per day, painters, $2.50 to $4 per day, and bricklayers $4 to $5 per day.

The increase in the Birmingham district may be studied as a type of the changes effected in the industrial centers of the South, as Birmingham is a great coal mining center and, with the exception of Pittsburgh, is the greatest iron ore district in the United States. On November 6, 1917, the average daily wage earnings of forty-five men was $5.49. On November 10, 1917, the average for seventy-five men was $5.30. One man was earning $10 a day, two $9 to $10 a day, five $8 to $9, six $7 to $8, ten $6 to $7, fourteen $5 to $6, thirty-two $4 to $5, nine $3 to $4, and six under $3. In the other coal and iron ore sections the earnings had been similarly increased.[1]

In Mississippi, largely a farming section, wages did not increase to the extent that they did in Alabama, but some increase was necessary to induce the negroes to remain on the plantations and towns to keep the industries going. In Greenville wages increased at first about ten per cent but this did not suffice to stop the migration, for, because of the scarcity of labor, factories and stores had to employ white porters, druggists had to deliver their own packages and firms had to resort to employing negro women. On the farms much of the crop was lost on account of the scarcity of labor. In Greenwood wages of common laborers increased from $1 and $1.25 to $1.75 per day. Clarksdale was also compelled to offer laborers more remuneration. Vicksburg found it necessary to increase the wages of negroes from $1.25 to $2 per day. There were laborers on steamboats who received $75 to $100 per month.

At Leland 500 to 1,000 men received $1.75 per day. The oil mills of Indianola raised the wages of the negroes from $1.50 to $2 per day. At Laurel the average daily wage was raised from $1.35 to $1.65, the maximum wage being $2. Wages increased at Meridian from 90 cents and $1.25 to $1.50 and $1.75 per day. The wholesale houses increased the compensation of their employes from $10 to $12 per week. From $1.10 in Hattiesburg the daily wage was raised to $1.75 and $2 per day. Wages in Jackson increased from $1 and $1.25 to $1.35 and $1.50 per day. In Natchez there was an increase of 25 per cent. On the whole, throughout the State there was an increase of from 10 to 30 per cent and in some instances of as much as 100 per cent.[2]

Throughout the South there was not only a change in policy as to the method of stopping the migration of the blacks to

[1] Work, *Report on the Migration from Alabama.*
[2] Johnson, *Report on the Migration from Mississippi.*

the North, but a change in the economic policy of the South. Southern business men and planters soon found out that it was impossible to treat the negro as a serf and began to deal with him as an actual employe entitled to his share of the returns from his labor. It was evident that it would be very much better to have the negroes as coworkers in a common cause than to have them abandon their occupations in the South, leaving their employers no opportunity to secure to themselves adequate income to keep them above want.

A more difficult change of attitude was that of the labor unions. They had for years been antagonistic to the negroes and had begun to drive them from many of the higher pursuits of labor which they had even from the days of slavery monopolized. The skilled negro laborer has gradually seen his chances grow less and less as the labor organizations have invaded the South. In the end, however, the trade unions have been compelled to yield, although complete economic freedom of the negro in the South is still a matter of prospect.

There was, too, a decided change in the attitude of the whole race toward the blacks. The white people could be more easily reached, and very soon there was brought about a better understanding between the races. Cities gave attention to the improvement of the sanitary condition of the negro sections, which had so long been neglected; negroes were invited to take part in the clean-up week; the Women's Health League called special meetings of colored women, conferred with them and urged them to organize community clubs. Committees of leading negroes dared to take up with their employers the questions of better accommodations and better treatment of negro labor. Members of these committees went before chambers of commerce to set forth their claims. Others dared boldly to explain to them that the negroes were leaving the South because they had not been given the treatment which should be accorded men.

Instead of expressing their indignation at such efforts on the part of the negroes, the whites listened to them attentively. Accordingly, joint meetings of the whites and blacks were held to hear frank statements of the case from speakers of both races. One of the most interesting of these meetings was the one held in Birmingham, Alabama. The negroes addressing the audience frankly declared that it was impossible to bring back from the North the migrants who were making good there, but that the immediate problem requiring solution was how to hold in the South those who had not gone. These negroes made it clear that it was impossible for negro leaders through the pulpit and press to check the movement, but that only through a change in the attitude of the whites to the blacks could the latter be made to feel that the Southland is safe for them.

Here we see the coming to pass of a thing long desired by those interested in the welfare of the South and long rejected by those who have always prized the peculiar interest of one race more highly than the welfare of all. White men, for the first time, were talking on the streets with negroes just as white men talk with each other. The merchants gave their negro patrons more attention and consideration. A prominent white man said, " I have never seen such changes as have come about within the last four months. I know of white men and negroes who have not dared to speak to one another on the streets to converse freely." The suspension of harsh treatment was so marked in some places that few negroes neglected to mention it. In Greenwood and Jackson, Mississippi, the police were instructed to curtail their practices of beating negroes. Several court cases in which negroes were involved terminated favorably for them. There followed directly after the exodus an attempt at more even handed justice, or at least some conciliatory measures were adopted. The authorities at Laurel, Mississippi, were cautioned to treat negroes better, so as to prevent their leaving. There is cited the case of a negro arrested on an ambiguous charge. He was assigned to the county chain gang and put to work on the roads. At this time the treatment in the courts was being urged by negroes as a reason for leaving. This negro's case was discussed. He was sent back from the county roads alone for a shovel. He did not return; and his return was not expected.[1]

[1] Johnson, *Report on the Migration from Mississippi.*

Conferences of negroes and whites in Mississippi emphasized the necessity of cooperation between the races for their common good. The whites said, to quote a negro laborer, " We must just get together." A negro said: " The dominant race is just a bit less dominant at present." " We are getting more consideration and appreciation," said another. From another quarter came the remark that " instead of the old proverbial accusation—shiftless and unreliable—negro labor is being heralded as ' the only dependable labor extant, etc.' " [1] A general review of the results made it clear that there was a disposition on the part of the white population to give some measure of those benefits, the denial of which was alleged as the cause of the exodus. For those who remained conditions were much more tolerable, although there appeared to persist a feeling of apprehension that these concessions would be retracted as soon as normal times returned. Some were of the opinion that the exodus was of more assistance to those negroes who stayed behind than to those who went away.

As a matter of fact, the white people in the South began to direct attention to serious work of reconstruction to make that section inviting to the negro. Bolivar county, Mississippi, as a direct result of the recommendation of the labor committee, made an appropriation of $25,000 toward an agricultural high school, the first of its kind in the State. The school boards of Coahoma and Adams counties have appointed Jeanes Foundation Supervisors and, in Coahoma county, promised a farm demonstration agent. They also made repairs on the school buildings in towns, and prominent whites have expressed a willingness to duplicate every dollar negroes raise for rural school improvements. A large planter in the Big Creek neighborhood has raised, together with his tenants, $1,000 for schools and the superintendent of schools has gone over the county urging planters to give land for negro schools. Two other large planters, whose tenants number into the hundreds, have made repairs on the schoolhouses on their plantations. The Mississippi Council of Defense passed a resolution calling upon the State

[1] Johnson, *Report on the Migration from Mississippi.*

to put a farm demonstrator and home economics agent to work in rural communities to make living conditions better in the effort to induce the people to stay.

This upheaval in the South, according to an investigator, will be helpful to all.

The decrease in the black population in those communities where the negroes outnumber the whites will remove the fear of negro domination. Many of the expensive precautions which the southern people have taken to keep the negroes down, much of the terrorism incited to restrain the blacks from self-assertion will no longer be considered necessary; for, having the excess in numbers on their side, the whites will finally rest assured that the negroes may be encouraged without any apprehension that they may develop enough power to subjugate or embarrass their former masters.

The negroes, too, are very much in demand in the South and the intelligent whites will gladly give them larger opportunities to attach them to that section, knowing that the blacks, once conscious of their power to move freely throughout the country wherever they may improve their condition, will never endure hardships like those formerly inflicted upon the race. The South is already learning that the negro is the most desirable labor for that section, that the persecution of negroes not only drives them out but makes the employment of labor such a problem that the South will not be an attractive section for capital. It will, therefore, be considered the duty of business men to secure protection to the negroes lest their ill treatment force them to migrate to the extent of bringing about a stagnation of business.

The exodus has driven home the truth that the prosperity of the South is at the mercy of the negro. Dependent on cheap labor, which the bulldozing whites will not readily furnish, the wealthy southerners must finally reach the position of regarding themselves and the negroes as having a community of interests which each must promote. " Nature itself in those States," Douglass said, "came to the rescue of the negro. He had labor, the South wanted it, and must have it or perish. Since he was free he could then give it, or withhold it; use it where he was, or take it elsewhere, as he pleased. His labor made him a slave and his labor could, if he would, make him free, comfortable and independent. It is more to him than either fire, sword, ballot boxes or bayonets. It touches the heart of the South through its pocket." Knowing that the negro has this silent weapon to be used against his employer or the community, the South is already giving the race better educational facilities, better railway accommodations, and will eventually, if the advocacy of certain southern newspapers be heeded, grant them political privileges. Wages in the South, therefore, have risen even in the extreme southwestern States, where there is an opportunity to import Mexican labor. Reduced to this extremity, the southern aristocrats have begun to lose some of their race prejudice, which has not hitherto yielded to reason or philanthropy.

Southern men are telling their neighbors that their section must abandon the policy of treating the negroes as a problem and construct a program for recognition rather than for repression. Meetings are, therefore, being held to find out what the negroes want and what may be done to keep them contented. They are told that the negro must be elevated, not exploited; that to make the South what it must needs be, the cooperation of all is needed to train and equip the men of all races for efficiency. The aim of all then must be to reform or get rid of the unfair proprietors who do not give their tenants a fair division of the returns from their labor. To this end the best whites and blacks are urged to come together to find a working basis for a systematic effort in the interest of all.[1]

Another evidence of the beneficent effects of the decrease in the population in the Black Belt of the South is the interest now almost generally manifested in the improvement of the negro quarters in southern cities. For a number of years science has made an appeal in behalf of the thoroughly clean city, knowing that since the germ does not draw the color line, a city can not be kept clean as long as a substantial portion of its citizens are crowded into one of its oldest and least desirable parts, neglected by the city and avoided by the whites. Doing now what science has hitherto failed to accomplish, this peculiar economic need of the negro in the South has brought about unusual changes in the appearance of southern cities. Darkened portions of urban districts have been lighted; streets in need of improvement have been paved; the water, light and gas systems have been extended to negro quarters and play grounds and parks have been provided for their amusement.

No less important has been the effect of the migration on the southern land tenure and the credit system, the very heart of the trouble in that section. For generations the negroes have borne it grievously that it has been difficult to obtain land for cultivation other than by paying exorbitant rents or giving their landlords an unusually large share of the crops. They have been further handicapped by the necessity of depending on such landlords to supply them with food and clothing at such exorbitant prices that their portion of the return from their labor has been usually exhausted before harvesting the crops. Cheated thus in the making of their contracts and in purchasing necessi-

[1] Woodson, *A Century of Negro Migration,* pp. 183-186.

ties, they have been but the prey of sharks and harpies bent upon keeping them in a state scarcely better than that of slavery. Southerners of foresight have, therefore, severely criticized this custom and, in a measure, have contributed to its decline. The press and the pulpit of the South are now urging the planters to abolish this system that the negroes may enjoy the fruits of their own labor. It is largely because of these urgent appeals in behalf of fair play, during the economic upheaval, that this legalized robbery is losing its hold in the South.

Recently welfare work among negroes has become a matter of much concern to the industries of the South in view of the exceptional efforts made along this line in the North. At the very beginning of the migration the National League on Urban Conditions among Negroes pointed out that firms wishing to retain negro laborers and to have them become efficient must give special attention to welfare work.[1] A considerable number of firms employing negro laborers in the North have used the services of negro welfare workers. Their duties have been to work with the men, study and interpret their wants and stand as a medium between the employer and his negro workmen. It has, therefore, come to be recognized in certain industrial centers in the South that money expended for this purpose is a good investment. Firms employing negro laborers in any considerable numbers have found out that they must be dealt with on the same general basis as white laborers. Among the industries in the South now looking out for their negro laborers in this respect are the Newport News Shipbuilding and Dry Dock Company, the American Cast Iron Pipe Company of Birmingham and the Tennessee Coal, Iron and Railroad Company.

These efforts take the form which usually characterize the operations of social workers. The laborers are cared for through the Y. M. C. A., the Y. W. C. A., the National Urban League

[1] At the National Conference, "The Problems of the Employment Manager in Industry" held at Rochester, New York, in May, 1918, considerable time was given to this question. In discussing psychology in the employment of negro workingmen Mr. E. K. Jones, Director of the Urban League, pointed out that negro laborers must be given not only good housing and recreation facilities but also the opportunity for advancement. "Give them," said he, "a chance to become foremen and to engage in all kinds of skill and delicate labor. This will inspire them and place new life in them."

and social settlement establishments. The attention of the welfare workers is directed to the improvement of living conditions through proper sanitation and medical attention. They are supplied with churches, school buildings and bath houses, enjoy the advantages of community singing, dramatic clubs and public games, and receive instruction in gardening, sewing and cooking. Better educational facilities are generally provided.

On the whole the South will profit by this migration. Such an upheaval was necessary to set up a reaction in the southern mind to enable its leaders of thought to look beyond themselves into the needs of the man far down. There is in progress, therefore, a reshaping of public opinion, in fact a peaceful revolution in a land cursed by slavery and handicapped by aristocracy. The tendency to maltreat the negroes without cause, the custom of arresting them for petty offenses and the institution of lynching have all been somewhat checked by this change in the attitude of the southern white man towards the negro. The check in the movement of the negroes to other parts may to some extent interfere with this development of the new public opinion in the South, but this movement has been so far reaching in its effect as to compel the thinking class of the South to construct and carry out a policy of fair play to provide against that day when that section may find itself again at the mercy of the laboring class of the negroes.

CHAPTER IX

The Situation in St. Louis

It will be both interesting and profitable to follow these migrants into their new homes in the North. Among the most interesting of these communities is the black colony in St. Louis. St. Louis is one of the first cities of the border States, a city first in the memory of the unsettled migrant when the North was mentioned. During a long period thousands had gone there, settled down for a while and moved on, largely to Illinois, a sort of promised land. Conservative estimates place the number of negro migrants who have remained there at 10,000. The number of migrants passing through this city, its reception of them, the living conditions provided and the community interest displayed in grappling with the problem are facts extremely necessary to an understanding of the readjustment of the migrants in the North.

The composition of the city's population is significant. It has a large foreign element. Of the foreign population Germans predominate, probably because of the brewery industry of the American white population. The southern whites are of longest residence and dominate the sentiment. The large industrial growth of the town, however, has brought great numbers of northern whites. The result is a sort of mixture of traditions. The apparent results of this mixture may be observed in these inconsistencies; separate schools, but common transportation facilities; separate playgrounds, but common bath houses; separate theaters and restaurants with the color line drawn as strictly as in the South.[1] There has been considerable migration of whites to this city from Kentucky, Tennessee, Alabama and Mississippi.

[1] A segregation law was passed by an overwhelming majority. Negroes secured an injunction and the matter rested there until the United States Supreme Court declared the segregation laws invalid.

As there are separate schools in St. Louis, the statistics of the St. Louis system may serve as an index to the sources and the increase of the negro population. The school population was known to increase approximately 500 between 1916 and 1917.[1] The school registration shows communities in which have settled numbers of families from the same State and even the same town. For example, in the vicinity of the Dessalines School in the 1700 block on 12th Street, North, Mississippi colonists are in preponderant majority. The towns represented here are located in the northeastern part of that State. In the vicinity of the L'Overture School are distinct colonies from west Tennessee and Alabama. On Lawton Avenue, another popular street, Mississippians also are in majority. What makes migration to St. Louis from these States easy is probably its convenient location and direct railway communication with them. There has been no influx from Texas and Florida.

How St. Louis secured her migrants makes an interesting story. The difficulty of apprehending labor agents can be appreciated when it is recalled that the most zealous efforts of authority in the majority of cases failed to find more than a trace of where they had been operating. It was asserted by many of the migrants to this city, however, that they had been approached at some time by agents. Large industrial plants located in the satellite city of St. Louis sent men to Cairo, a junction point, to meet incoming trains and make offers. There developed a competition for men. They were first induced to accept jobs in smaller towns, but lack of recreational facilities and amusements and the monotony of life attracted them to the bright lights of St. Louis. The large alien population of this city at the beginning of the war made some employers anxious about the safety of their plants. The brick yards had been employing foreigners exclusively. When war began so many left that it was felt that their business was in danger. They advertised for 3,000 negroes, promising them $2.35 per day. The railroad construction companies sent out men to attract negroes to the city. They assert, however, that their

[1] St. Louis School Reports, 1916 and 1917.

agents solicited men only after they had started for the North.[1]

The industries of St. Louis had much to do with the migration. In this city there are more than twenty breweries. None of these employ negroes. St. Louis also has a large shoe industry. In this line no negroes are employed. A short while ago a large steel plant employing foreigners in large numbers had a strike. The strike was settled but the management took precautions against its repetition. For each white person employed a negro was placed on a corresponding job. This parallel extended from unskilled work to the highest skilled pursuits. The assumption was that a strike, should it recur, could not cripple their industry entirely. About 80 per cent of the employes of the brick yards, 50 per cent of the employes of the packing houses, 50 per cent of the employes of the American Car and Foundry Company are negroes. The terra cotta works, electrical plants, united railways and a number of other foundries employ negroes in large numbers.[2]

The range of wages for unskilled work is $2.25 to $3.35 per day, with an average wage of about $2.75. For some skilled work negroes receive from 35 cents to 50 cents an hour. Wages differ even between St. Louis and East St. Louis, because of a difference in the types of industries in the two cities. Domestic service has been literally drained, and wages here have been forced upwards to approximate in some measure the increase in other lines.

The housing facilities for negroes, though not the best, are superior to such accommodations in most southern cities. There are about six communities in which the negroes are in the majority. Houses here are as a rule old, having been occupied by whites before they were turned over to negroes. Before the migration to the city, property owners reported that they could not keep their houses rented half of the year. According to the statements of real estate men, entire blocks stood vacant, and many vacant houses, after windows had been broken and plumbing stolen, were wrecked to avoid paying taxes on them.

[1] Johnson, *Report on the Migration to St. Louis.*
[2] *Ibid.*

Up to the period of the riot in East St. Louis, houses were easily available. The only congestion experienced at all followed the overnight increase of 7,000 negroes from East St. Louis, after the riot. Rents then jumped 25 per cent, but normal conditions soon prevailed. Sanitation is poor, but the women coming from the South, in the opinion of a reputable physician of the city, are good housewives. New blacks have been added to all of the negro residential blocks. In the tenement district there have been no changes. The select negro residential section is the abandoned residential district of the whites. Few new houses have been built. An increase of rent from $5 to $10 per month is usually the sequel of the turning over of a house to negroes.

Community interest in the situation was at first dormant but not entirely lacking. The migration was well under way before there was any organization to make an adjustment in this unusual situation. Interested individuals made sporadic efforts to bring pressure to bear here and there, but the situation was not really appreciated until the outbreak in East St. Louis. There is an active branch of the National Association for the Advancement of Colored People, and just recently there has been established a branch of the National League on Urban Conditions among Negroes to deal with the peculiarly local problems.[1]

East St. Louis, another attractive center for the migrants, is unique among northern industrial cities. It is an industrial offshoot of St. Louis, which has outstripped its parent in expansion. Its geographical advantage has made it a formidable rival even with its less developed civic institutions. Perched on the banks of the Mississippi River, with twenty-seven railroads radiating from it, within easy reach of the coal mines, there has been made possible a rapid and uneven growth. It has doubled its population for three successive decades. Revolving around this overgrown center are a number of small towns: Brooklyn, Lovejoy, Belleville, Venice, Granite City and Madison. Its plant owners live in St. Louis and other cities,

[1] *Reports of the National Urban League*, 1916, 1917.

and consequently have little civic interest in East St. Louis. Land is cheaper, taxes are low. In fact, some of the largest concerns have been accused of evading them entirely. It has been artificially fed and, in process of growth, there have been irregularities in the structure of the community which eventually culminated in the greatest disgrace of the North, the massacre of about one hundred negroes.

Fifty years ago before the river dividing St. Louis from East St. Louis was bridged, men rowed over from St. Louis for their cock fights, dog fights and prize fights. Escaped prisoners found a haven there. The town was called "The Bloody Isle." The older population is made up of whites from West Tennessee, Mississippi, Kentucky and Georgia. The men who have risen to political prominence in the city are for the most part saloon keepers. As many as 100 saloons flourished in the town before the riot. The city government has always been bad. The attitude of the citizenry appeared to be that of passive acceptance of conditions which must not be interfered with. As an example of the state of mind, much surprise was manifested when an investigation of the rioting was begun. Criminals have been known to buy immunity. The mayor was assassinated some time ago and little or no effort was made to punish his murderers.

Long before an influx was felt, it had been foreseen and mentioned by several men, most notably, Mr. Charles Nagel, Secretary of Commerce and Labor under President Taft. The East St. Louis plants had been going to Ellis Island for laborers. When this supply was checked, steps were taken to secure negroes. Agents were sent to Cairo to get men en route further North. One advertisement which appeared in a Texas paper promised negroes $3.05 a day and houses. It is estimated that as a result of this beckoning the increase in population due to the migration was 5,000. A number of other negro migrants, however, work in East St. Louis and live in St. Louis, Lovejoy and Brooklyn, a negro town. The school registration of the city showed that the largest numbers of these blacks came from Mississippi and West Tennessee. Despite the advertisement for men in Texas newspapers, few came to this city from that State.[1]

The industries requiring the labor of these negroes were numerous. The packing plants of Swift, Armour, Nelson and Morris employ large numbers of negroes. In some of the unskilled departments fifty per cent of the employes are black. The Aluminum Ore Works employs about 600 blacks and 1,000 whites. This is the plant in which occurred the strike which in a measure precipitated the riot. The Missouri Malleable Iron Works makes it a policy to keep three classes of men at work and as nearly equal numerically as possible. The usual division is one-third foreign whites, one-third American whites and one-third blacks. The theory is that these three elements will not unite to strike. Negroes are also employed in the glass works, cotton presses and transfer yards. Their wages for unskilled work ranges from $2.75 to $3.75 generally for eight hours a day. Semiskilled work pays from 35 cents to 50 cents an hour.

The housing of the negro migrants was one of the most perplexing problems in East St. Louis. The type of houses available for negroes, before being burned during the riot, were small dilapidated cottages. Congestion, of course, was a problem which accompanied the influx of negroes. The incoming population, consisting largely of lodgers, was a misfit in the small cottages designed for families, and they were generally neglected by the tenant and by the local authorities. The segregated vice district was located in the negro locality. The crowding which followed the influx forced some few negroes into the white localities. Against this invasion there was strong opposition which culminated in trouble.[2]

The roots of the fateful horror that made East St. Louis notorious, however, are to be found largely in a no less notorious civic structure. Politics of a shady nature was the handmaiden of the local administration. The human fabric of the town was made up of sad types of rough, questionable characters,

[1] Johnson, *Report on the Migration to St. Louis.*
[2] See *Congressional Report on the Massacre of East St. Louis.*

drawn to the town by its industries and the money that flowed from them. There was a large criminal element. These lived in a little corner of the town, where was located also the segregated vice district. Negroes were interested in politics. In fact, they were a considerable factor and succeeded in placing in office several black men of their choice.

Trouble started at the Aluminum Ore Works which employed a large number of whites and blacks. In February of 1917 the men struck while working on government contracts. Immediately, it is claimed, negroes were sought for in other States to take their places. An adjustment was made, but it lasted only a short while. Then followed a second strike at which the employers balked. In this they felt reasonably secure for negroes were then pouring into the city from the South during the spring exodus. There followed numerous evidences of brooding conflict such as insults on the street cars, comments and excitement over the daily arrival of large numbers from the South. On one day three hundred are said to have arrived. Standing on the streets, waiting for cars, lost in wandering about the streets searching for homes, the negroes presented a helpless group. The search for homes carried them into the most undesirable sections. Here the scraggy edges of society met. The traditional attitude of unionists toward negroes began to assert itself. Fear that such large numbers would weaken present and subsequent demands aroused considerable opposition to their presence. Meetings were held, exciting speeches were made and street fights became common. The East St. Louis *Journal* is said to have printed a series of articles under the caption, "Make East St. Louis a Lily White Town." It was a simple matter of touching off the smoldering tinder. In the riot that followed over a hundred negroes were killed. These, for the most part lived away from the places of the most violent disturbances, and were returning home, unconscious of the fate that awaited them. The riot has recently been subject to a congressional investigation, but few convictions resulted and those whites convicted escaped serious punishment.[1]

[1] See *Congressional Report on the Massacre of East St. Louis.*

CHAPTER X

Chicago and Its Environs

Chicago, the metropolis of the West, remembered in the South since the World's Fair as a far-away city of hope from which come all grea. things; unceasingly advertised through its tremendous mail order and clothing houses, schools and industries until it became a synonym for the " North," was the mouth of the stream of negroes from the South. It attracted all types of men, brought them in, encouraged them and cared for them because it needed them. It is estimated that within the period of eighteen months beginning January, 1916, more than fifty thousand negroes entered the city. This estimate was based on averages taken from actual count of daily arrivals.

There were at work in this city a number of agencies which served to stimulate the movement. The stock yards were sorely in need of men. It was reported that they had emissaries in the South. Whether it is true or not, it is a fact that it was most widely advertised throughout the States of Mississippi and Louisiana that employment could easily be secured in the Chicago stock yards district. The report was circulated that fifty thousand men were needed, and the packers were providing houses for migrants and caring for them until they had established themselves. The Illinois Central Railroad brought hundreds on free transportation with the understanding that the men would enter the employ of the company. The radical negro newspapers published here urged negroes to leave the South and promised employment and protection. It is indeed little wonder that Chicago received so great a number.

The most favorable aspect of their condition in their new home is their opportunity to earn money. Coming from the South, where they were accustomed to work for a few cents a day or a few dollars a week, to an industrial center where they can now earn as much in an hour or a day, they have the feeling that this city is really the land overflowing with milk and honey. In the occupations in which they are now employed, many of them are engaged at skilled labor, receiving the same and, in some cases, greater compensation than was paid white men in such positions prior to the outbreak of the war. Talking with a number of them the investigator obtained such information as, that men were working at the Wilson Packing House and receiving $3 a day; at the Marks Manufacturing Company for $3.75; as lumber stackers at $4 a day, at one of the rolling mills for $25 a week, and on the railroads at $125 a month. The large majority of these migrants are engaged in the packing houses of Chicago where they are employed to do all sorts of skilled and unskilled labor with the corresponding compensation.[1]

It was soon discovered that the needs of the migrants could not all be supplied by money. Something had to be done for their social welfare. Various agencies assisted in caring for the needs of the 25,000 or more negro migrants who, it is estimated, have come to Chicago within three years. The Chicago Renting Agents' Association appointed a special committee to study the problems of housing them and to confer with leaders in civic organization and with representative negroes. The Cook County Association considered the question of appointing some one to do Sunday School work exclusively among the newcomers. The Housing Committee of the Chicago Women's Club arranged for an intensive survey of housing conditions. The negroes themselves organized to help the recently arrived members of the race. Negro ministers, lawyers, physicians and social workers cooperated in handling the problem through churches, Sunday Schools and in other ways.[2]

The negroes residing in Chicago, who came from particular States in the South organized clubs to look after the migrants from their own States. The result was that an Alabama Club, a Georgia Club, Mississippi Club, Tennessee Club and so on

[1] Johnson, *Report on the Migration to Chicago.*
[2] *Ibid.*

were formed. Committees from these clubs met the train and helped the newcomers to find homes and work. The chief agency in handling the migrant situation in Chicago was the local branch of the National League on Urban Conditions among Negroes. The work which the league did for the migrants as set forth in the report of 1917 was of three kinds: employment, housing and adjustment or assimilation. The policy of the Urban League with regard to employment was to find and, where possible, to open new occupations hitherto denied negroes. The housing problem was urgent. The most that the league was able to do thus far was to find lodging, to assist in finding houses. Lodging accommodations for more than 400 individuals were personally inspected by several women volunteers. It is impossible to do much else short of the construction of apartments for families and for single men.

The league's first efforts to assimilate the new people started with their entrance to the city. To see that they received proper directions upon reaching the railroad station was an important task. It was able to secure the services of a volunteer travelers' aid society. This agent met trains and directed migrants to destinations when they had addresses of relatives and friends. In the absence of such they were sent to proper homes for lodging, and to the league office for employment.

The great majority of negroes in Chicago live in a limited area known as the South Side. State Street is the thoroughfare. It is the black belt of the city. This segregation is aided on one hand by the difficulty of securing houses in other sections of the city, and on the other, by the desire of negroes to live where they have greatest political strength. Previous to the migration, hundreds of houses stood vacant in the sections of the district west of State Street from which they had moved only a few years before, when it was found that better homes were available. The presence of negroes in an exclusively white locality usually brought forth loud protests and frequently ended in the abandonment of the block by whites. The old district lying west of State Street held the worst type of houses. It was also in disrepute because of its proximity to the old segregated vice area. The newcomers, unacquainted with its reputation, found no hesitancy in moving in until better homes could be secured.

Congestion has been a serious problem only during short periods when the influx was greater than the city's immediate capacity for distributing them. During the summer of 1917 this was the situation. A canvass of real estate dealers supplying houses for negroes conducted by the Chicago Urban League revealed the fact that on a single day there were 664 negro applicants for houses, and only 50 supplied,. while there were 97 houses advertised for rent. In some instances as many as ten persons were listed for a single house. This condition did not continue long. There were counted thirty-six new localities opening up to negroes within three months. These localities were formerly white.

An accompaniment to this congestion was the increase in rents of from 5 to 30 per cent and sometimes as high as 50 per cent. This was explained by landlords as a return to former standards after the property had depreciated through the coming in of negroes. A more detailed study of living conditions among the migrants in Chicago was made by a student of the School of Civics and Philanthropy. The study included 75 families of less than a year's residence. In the group were 60 married couples, 128 children, eight women and nine married men with families in the South.

How this large group—265 persons—fresh from a region where life is enlivened by a mild climate and ample space was to find living quarters in an overcrowded section of two Chicago blocks was a problem of many aspects. A single furnished room, rented by the week, provided the solution for each of 41 families, while 24 families rented homes by the month, four families occupied two rooms each. In some instances, this meant overcrowding so serious as to threaten morals and health. The Urban League interested corporations and capitalists in the construction of modern apartment houses with small individual apartments. It endeavored also to have the city see the necessity of preventing occupancy of the physically unfit houses.

The league conducted a campaign to educate the masses in regard to housing, and payment of exorbitant rents was discouraged. The various city departments were asked to enforce ordinances in negro neighborhoods. In this way the league tried to reduce overcrowding and extortionate rentals.

All of the arrivals here did not stay. They were only temporary guests awaiting the opportunity to proceed further and settle in surrounding cities and towns. This tendency appears to have been to reach those fields offering the highest wages and most permanent prospects. With Chicago as a center there are within a radius of from one hundred to one hundred and fifty miles a number of smaller industrial centers—suburbs of Chicago in which enterprises have sprung up because of the nearness to the unexcelled shipping and other facilities which Chicago furnished. A great many of the migrants who came to Chicago found employment in these satellite places.[1]

One of these towns was Rockford, a city of about 55,000 people before Camp Grant began to add to its population. It is estimated that there were about 1,500 negroes in Rockford, 1,000 of whom came in during 1916 and 1917. The Rockford Malleable Iron Company, which never hired more than five or six negroes until two years ago, has nearly one hundred in its employ. A timekeeper, five inspectors, a machinist, a porter, three foremen and twenty of the molders are negroes. The Free Sewing Machine Company, Emerson and Birmingham, the Trahern Pump Company and the two knitting factories began also to employ negroes. The standard wage prevailed, and, while the unskilled work was largely given to the negroes, there were instances when opportunity was given for them to follow pursuits requiring skill.

Housing showed every evidence of congestion. The city was unprepared for the unprecedented increase in population necessitated by the demands of its factories for men to produce munitions of war. The workingmen, however, were soon better provided for than in some other cities. The Rockford Malleable

---

[1] The Detroit branch of the Urban League reported, for example, that a great percentage of its applicants for work were from Chicago.

Iron Company conducted two houses for the accommodation of its employes and rented several smaller ones.[1] This company had recently purchased a large acreage and was considering the advisability of building houses for its employes, including the negro migrants. The Emerson and Birmingham Company and the Sewing Machine Company had similar plans under advisement.

The Rockford Malleable Iron Company was the first to use negroes. In the fall of 1916 the first negro employes were brought in from Canton, Illinois, through a Mr. Robinson then employed by the company as a molder. There were nine molders in the group. At brief intervals Tuskegee sent up four, then five, then eight and then six men, most of whom had had training in machinery and molding. The total number of Tuskegee boys was 32. Robinson also brought men from Metropolis, Illinois, and from Kankakee. He made a trip through Alabama and brought up 15 or 16. Most of these were laborers. Seven laborers came as a result of correspondence with a physician from Des Moines, Iowa. From Christiansburg, Virginia, the only negro blacksmith came. The Urban League also sent up some men from Chicago. The company was so pleased with the men's service that they called upon the Urban League for more men and placed in its hands a fund for their railroad expenses.[2]

Negroes were promoted from time to time and were used in every department of the shop. One of the men was an inspector. Two new machines turning out work faster than any other machine were turned over to the negroes. All of them were given steady work without being forced to lay off, and their wages were increased. Street car companies and officials in Rockford have congratulated the men upon their conduct. Two of the men who came up from the South were purchasing property.

When the increase in negro population became noticeable, a

[1] The two large houses accommodated fifty to sixty men. One of these was known as the Tuskegee Club House and housed only men from Tuskegee Institute.

[2] Johnson, *Report on the Migration to Chicago.*

good deal of discrimination appeared in public places. The mayor of the city, therefore, called a conference of the Chamber of Commerce, of representatives from Camp Grant, hotels, skating rinks and other public places and read the civil rights law to them. He gave them to understand that Rockford would not stand for discrimination between races. When some of the conferees thought they would like to have separate tables in the restaurants the mayor opposed them and insisted that there should be no such treatment. One restaurant, which displayed a sign, "We do not cater to colored trade," was given orders by the Chief of Police to take it down in fifteen minutes, when his deputy would arrive with instructions to carry out the law in case the sign was not removed.

Waukegan, a town thirty miles northwest of Chicago, with a total population of about 22,000 has approximately 400 negroes, where two years ago there were about 275. The Wilder Tanning Company and the American Steel and Wire Company employed the largest number of these negroes. These firms worked about 60 and 80 respectively. Smaller numbers were employed by the Gas Company, the Calk Mill, the Cyclone Fence Company, the Northwestern Railroad freight house and a bed spring factory and several were working at the Great Lakes Naval Training Station. A few found employment as porters in barber shops and theaters. At the Wilder Tanning Company and the American Steel and Wire Company, opportunity was given negroes to do semiskilled work. The former was working negroes into every branch of its industry. The average daily wage here was about $3.[1]

[1] In May, 1917, the Sherman House on Genesee Street in the heart of the city became a negro hotel. It has 19 bedrooms and accommodates 35 men. It was poorly managed and dirty. A barber shop, pool room and dining room were run in connection with it and were also poorly managed. The manager of the hotel is one of the newcomers. A rooming house and dance hall for negroes is operated in another section of the city. The Wilder Tanning Company was building a hotel for 50 single men and individual houses of five, six, seven and eight rooms for families. Houses for white workmen were to be built by the company after these were completed. Lawrence Wilder, president of the company, stated that the building of these houses was no "experiment." "They are being put up to stay." Hot and cold water, hot air, heat, electric lights, and shower baths will be in the hotel. Single rooms will rent for $1.25, double rooms $2.50 per week. No women will be permitted to live in the hotel. A social room will be

The secretary of the Chamber of Commerce believed that the influx did not cause anything more than a ripple on the surface. He said: " I cover everything when I say that, no apparent increase in crime; no trouble among themselves; no race friction." Theaters began to discriminate, but soon ceased. The proprietor of the Sheridan Club stated that he took a group of men to one theater which had shown signs of discrimination. Each man was told to purchase his own ticket. The owner observing the scheme admitted them. Very few restaurants refuse to serve negroes. Only one openly segregated them to a particular part of the dining-room. Absolutely no trouble was experienced in the schools. The police commissioner sees that the negroes have the protection of the law.

East Chicago, an industrial center located about twenty-five miles from Chicago with a population now made up in large part of Hungarians, Poles, Italians and negroes, had only one negro family in 1915. During the month of August, 1916, about 150 negroes came and others soon followed. At present there are about 75 families, 35 or 40 children of school age and about 450 men working in the industrial plants. The majority of these newcomers were from the rural districts of Alabama and Georgia, with a few from Mississippi. A large number of negroes, moreover, live in Indiana Harbor and in Chicago and work in East Chicago.[1]

Some of the people went to Indiana Harbor for church serv-

within easy access of all occupants. No meals will be served at the hotel, but will be served at the plant. The houses will be one and two stories and can be purchased on a monthly basis. A street car line will connect the plant and the subdivision.

Before the influx the Cyclone Fence Company and the Calk Mill Company were said to have sworn never to employ negro labor. The Wilder Tanning Company and the American Steel and Wire Company have standing invitations for negro men with references.—Johnson, *Report on the Migration to Chicago.*

[1] They were employed by the Gasselli Chemical Company, Goldsmiths Detinning Company, the International Lead Refining Company, the United States Reduction Company, the United States Refining Company, Hobson and Walker's Brick Yard, the Inland Steel Foundry, Interstate Mill, the Cudahy Soap Factory and the Republic Rolling Mill. The Hobson and Walker's Brick Yard employed 200 and provided houses within the yards for the families of the workmen. The International Lead Refining Company provided lodging for its men in remodeled box cars. Wages for ordinary labor ranged from $2.50 to $4.50 per day. This did not include the amount

ices. During the summer of 1917, an attempt was made to organize a church, but it was unsuccessful and almost excited a racial conflict. The negroes from Alabama and Georgia complained about the wickedness of East Chicago, and declared their intentions of going home, " where they can sing without appearing strange, and where they can hear somebody else pray besides themselves." Few racial clashes, however, have followed. A strike which occurred at Gasselli's Chemical Company was at first thought to be a protest of the foreigners against the 80 negroes employed there. Nothing serious developed from it. The only apparent dangers were in thoughtlessness on the part of negroes in their conduct. They were too badly needed in industry to be harshly treated either by the foreigners or their employers.[1]

In Beloit, Wisconsin, as in other cities, it was impossible to find out with any degree of accuracy the approximate number of negroes. Estimates of the number ranged from 700 to 2,000, whereas, before the influx, the black population was as low as 200. The total population of Beloit is about 20,000. There are now two negro churches, a Baptist and an African Methodist Episcopal. The Baptist church was said to be made up entirely of new people. Beloit did not have a negro Baptist

that might be made by overtime work. The brick yard employed negroes for unskilled work at 35 cents an hour. A few skilled negroes employed were receiving from $4.75 to $7 a day.

Negroes are fairly well scattered throughout the foreign residential section. A small area known as "Oklahoma" or "Calumet" had perhaps the largest number. The houses were overcrowded, dark, insanitary, without privacy and generally unattractive. All of the rooms were sleeping rooms, usually with two beds in a room accommodating six men. Rent was high, and ranged from $15 to $25 a month for four and five room flats in very unattractive buildings. Single lodgers paid from $1.50 to $1.75 a week. Restaurant rates were exorbitant and food was so high that many of the families bought their provisions in Chicago.

There were no churches or in fact any wholesome social institutions in town. There were many flourishing saloons. There was one colored pool room, and one colored restaurant. On occasions, a hall belonging to the whites was used for dances and socials.—Johnson, *Report on the Migration to Chicago.*

[1] Following each pay day from twenty to thirty negroes left for their homes in the South. Some returned when their funds were about exhausted and worked five or six months more. Others remained at home for the winter. "It was expected that the brick yard would lose a very large number on the 8th of November. On the 15th of December another large contingent leaves for the South."—Johnson, *Report on the Migration to Chicago.*

preacher until the migration, and had no negro physicians. Prior to the influx there was little discrimination, except in some of the restaurants and occasionally in the theaters. One negro was working at the post office, and another at the railroad station. Aside from these, the negro men were practically all laborers and porters.

As is true in most small cities, one company took the initiative in sending for men from the South. The Fairbanks Morse Company was the pioneer corporation in this respect in Beloit. This company hires at present 200 men. ·Most of these came from Mississippi. In fact, Albany and Pontotoc, small towns in Mississippi, are said to have dumped their entire population in Beloit. A few from Memphis, Tennessee, were employed there but the company preferred Mississippians, and had agents at work in that State getting men for its plant. It was said to be fair in its treatment of negroes and to pay the standard wages.[1]

Milwaukee was one of the ready recipients of negro migrants from other points in the North. Following the outbreak of the war, the consequent cessation of foreign immigration and the withdrawal of a number of aliens from the labor market to follow their national colors, a large demand for negro labor was for the first time created. Milwaukee apparently could not attract voluntary migration, and the larger plants were forced to import some 1,200 southern negroes to man their industries. In 1910, the city had a negro population of 980. There are now in Milwaukee about 2,700 negroes of whom 1,500 are

---

[1] There was great congestion in housing, as the negroes were restricted to certain sections with homes usually kept in insanitary condition. A very large housing plan of the company met with objection on the part of the white citizens who sent in a petition to the ·City Council against building houses for negroes. The City Council said they wanted the housing property for park purposes. The matter was taken to court. The Council condemned the property but failed to sustain the belief that it was needed for a park. Through various methods of red tape and legal procedure the matter was delayed. The company then built houses on a smaller scale. The plans included two apartment houses that would accommodate six families each. There were also in the course of erection houses for men with families to take the place of some improvised huts which the company had found necessary to use to facilitate the work of the men.—Johnson, *Report on the Migration to Chicago.*

newcomers, not only from the South, but from the adjacent States of Illinois, Iowa, Michigan and Minnesota.[1]

This migration to Milwaukee caused a number of difficulties. The first difficulty to arise was in the relationship of the migrant to the old residents of the city. Like the newly arrived foreigners they lived rather " close lives," had little contact with the people of the community and as a consequence were slow in changing their southern standards. This lack of contact was registered in the slight attendance in the colored churches, which are by far the most common medium of personal contact among negroes. The leading pastors and two others who have made unsuccessful attempts to establish churches complained that the newcomers, although accustomed to going to church in their old homes, " strayed from the fold " in the large city. There was also a certain unmistakable reticence on the part of the newcomers with respect to the negroes of longer residence. The new arrivals were at times suspicious of the motives of the older residents, and resented being advised how to conduct themselves. They were for the most part not in touch with any civic agency. The migrants, therefore, came into contact with the lower element. The recreations and amusements of the newcomers were those which the social outcasts furnished them.[2]

Another anomaly was to be observed in the motives behind the migration. The most recent European immigrants, unfamiliar with the character of the plants, having strong bodies and a disposition to work, are engaged as unskilled laborers. They do not, of course, remain at this level, but are continually pushed forward by later comers. The men who filled these lower positions were not the best type of foreigners. When the war began and this influx from Europe was stopped, it was for these positions that the plants were forced to seek men. Negroes were sought in the South, but, unfortunately, the emphasis was placed on quantity and not quality. Those who were able to move on shortest notice, those with few responsibilities

---

[1] Before 1910, 114 persons had arrived; between 1911 and 1915, 72; during 1916, 74; durng 1917, 102; and during 1918, 40 persons had arrived.
[2] Johnson, *Report on the Migration to Chicago.*

and few interests at home, were snapped up by the labor agents. This blunder has also registered itself in the records of the city and the character of the negro migrants. This was probably due to the fact that little is known of Milwaukee in the South. Unlike Chicago, Detroit, New York and other northern cities, it was not a popular destination for voluntary migration. Agents who scoured the South for men testified that in a large number of cases the first question asked was whether or not Milwaukee was a wet town, for the southern States have prohibited the sale of liquor. While Chicago got advertisement in the South through its great mail order business, most of what was known of Milwaukee related to its breweries.

The negroes here, however, had numerous industrial opportunities. The manner in which the trades suddenly opened up to them made it difficult to ascertain the number of negroes so engaged. An intensive study of a neighborhood showed a much wider variety of skilled negro laborers and brought to light the cases of many not otherwise known. One man in touch with the iron workers of the city ventured the statement that there were perhaps 75 negroes engaged in skilled work in the iron and steel industries of the city. In a large number of other plants one or two negroes had succeeded in finding skilled employment. Firms known to employ negroes in the capacity of skilled workmen are the Plankington Packing Company, Wehr Steel and Machine Shops, the National Malleable Iron Works, A. J. Lindeman-Hoverson Company and the Milwaukee Coke and Gas Company. For the most part skilled negroes are butchers and molders.[1]

In the case of negroes from the South with trades, however, there arose a situation which is seldom fully appreciated. A man in the South may be skilled in such an independent trade as shoemaking, tailoring, carpentry and the like, but in a northern city with its highly specialized industrial processes and divisions of labor, he must learn over again what he thought he had mastered, or abandon his trade entirely and seek employment in unskilled lines. The wages for skilled work were for

[1] Johnson, *Report on the Migration to Chicago.*

butchers, 55 to 64 cents an hour; for steel molders, 35 to 47 cents an hour; for firemen, $27 per week; for chauffeurs, $15 to $30 a week; for shoemakers, $20 a week; stationary firemen, $24 a week. The mass of negroes, men and women, gainfully employed in the city was made up of manual laborers. Vacancies for negroes in industry were made at the bottom. The range of occupations in unskilled work, however, was fairly wide. They were packing house employes, muckers, tannery laborers, street construction workers, dock hands and foundry laborers. Their wages were for foundry laborers, 32½ cents to 35 cents an hour; for muckers, $28 a week; for tannery laborers, $24 a week; dock hands, 60 cents an hour; and for packing house laborers, 43 cents an hour (male), and 30½ cents an hour (female). There were also porters in stores and janitors whose weekly wages averaged between $15 and $18 per week.

Several firms made strenuous efforts to induce laborers to come from the South. The Pfister-Vogel Company employed a negro to secure them for this purpose, and made preparation for their lodging and board. This representative stated that he was responsible for the presence of about 300 negroes in the city. Reverend J. S. Woods of the Booker T. Washington social settlement, who was actively engaged in assisting the plants, asserted that he had placed over 400. The Albert Trostel Company paid transportation for nearly 100 men.

The principal industries employing negroes with the number employed were about as follows:[1]

Firm	Number Male	Female
Plankington Packing Co.	78	10
Albert Trostel Leather Co.	75	30
Faulk's Manufacturing Co.	34	
Hoffman Manufacturing Co.	2	
Tunnell Construction Co.	10	
Milwaukee Coke and Gas Co.	38	
Pfister-Vogel Tannery	75	
A. J. Lindeman-Hoverson Co.	13	
National Malleable Iron Co.	22	
Solvay Steel Castings Co.	24	
Allis Chalmers	70	

[1] Johnson, *Report on the Migration to Chicago.*

On December 1, 1917, the Plankington Packing Company employed 93 men and 27 women. The Pfister-Vogel Company had only 75 men in its employ. This company, however, within 18 months had employed 300 negroes from the South.

Concerning the range of wages for negroes in these lines the data provided by these firms gave some means of information.

Firms	Male	Female
Plankington Packing Co.	43c to 64c an hour	30½c an hour
Faulk's Manufacturing Co. ...	35c to 47c an hour	
Hoffman Manufacturing Co. .	32½c an hour	
Tunnell Construction Co.	$4 a day	
Albert Trostel Co.	40c an hour	30c an hour
Milwaukee Coke and Gas Co.	$3.67 to $4.79 a day.......	
A. J. Lindeman-Hoverson Co.	$3 to $5 a day	
National Malleable Iron Co. ..	35c an hour to $4 a day.....	
Pfister-Vogel Tannery	$22 to $24 a week..........	

The quality of the workingmen is of interest both to the employers and social workers. To get uniform data employers were asked the principal faults and principal merits of their negro workmen. To the question, " What are the principal faults of your negro workmen? " these answers were given: [1]

None that predominate.

The principal fault of negro workmen is, they are slow and very hard to please.

Not good on rapid moving machinery, have not had mechanical training; slow; not stable.

Inclined to be irregular in attendance to work.

Very unsteady.

Leave in summertime for road work.

To the question, " What are the principal merits of your negro workmen? " these answers were given:

They are superior to foreign labor because they readily understand what you try to tell them.

Loyalty, willingness, cheerfulness.

The skilled men stick and are good workmen.

Generally speaking they are agreeable workmen.

Quicker, huskier, and can stand more heat than other workmen.

[1] Johnson, *Report on the Migration to Chicago.*

The attitude of white and black workmen toward one another in none of the plants visited presented anything like a serious situation. The following ·are answers to questions relating to this sentiment as returned by the important industries:[1]

No feeling—no complaints—no comments.

White and black get along well. There was a little trouble some time ago between a Jewish foreman and his negro workmen. All the negroes quit. The matter was investigated and the foreman discharged.

Good.

The relations are favorable, although negroes appear a bit clannish.

Good fellowship prevails.

Negroes do not stay long enough to get acquainted.

Good in most cases. Very little opposition. They are working as helpers with whites. Few objections.

As a final effort to get the opinion of employers themselves concerning the best means of improving their labor, a suggestion from them on this matter was solicited. Their views are subjoined:[2]

A rather broad question and one that could only be answered after considerable study. Believe the great trouble with negro labor has been the fact that a poor class of negroes has been employed by many. We have a good lot of workers now.

Some means should be devised to get them away from their general shiftless ways.

Education.

As a negro can be very contented and happy on very little, if their living conditions were improved and the desire created in them to improve their condition, this would be a help towards encouragement in bettering their social condition. In fact, we feel that anything that would help to better the social attention of the negro would make him a better workman.

Better housing and supervision through some responsible organization. Some way to keep sympathetic watch over them.

Without doubt there is an element of truth in each of these comments. It is unquestionably true that a large number of these men register by their actions instability, irregularity and general shiftlessness. Some of these cases are inexcusable, and

[1] Johnson, *Report on the Migration to Chicago.*
[2] *Ibid.*

the only reason for their connection with the industry is the fact that they were brought from the South, where they were voluntarily idle, by agents of employers. The importation merely shifted the scene of their deliberate loafing and spasmodic contact with work.

Employers in all of the plants know that they have had difficulty in holding their negro labor, but do not know why. Most of the men willing to leave the city were unmarried men with few responsibilities. These are the ones who found employment there and, being dissatisfied, quit. The highest negro labor turnover was in the leather factories. But for this there was a reason. The only employment permitted negroes there was wet and very disagreeable beam work, and at wages not in excess of those paid by neighboring plants with a different grade of work. Inquiries among laboring men reveal reasons plausible indeed to the laborers themselves, which in many cases would have been found reasonable also by the employers.

It is generally known that all classes of labor of all nationalities are in an unsettled state. Shifting to the higher paid industries is common. In consequence the disagreeable and poorly paid ones have suffered. The instability of negroes, especially in those industries that have been so hard pressed as to find it necessary to go South for men, is not so much a group characteristic as an expression of present tendencies in labor generally.

Reasons of a more intimate nature advanced by the men for changing jobs are numerous. Among these are dissatisfaction with the treatment of petty white bosses, the necessity for ready money for the care of their families, the distance of the plants from the district in which the negro workmen live [1] and the unpleasant indoor work in certain factories.

The social condition of negroes in Milwaukee is not alarming. There are indicated, however, unmistakable maladjustments

[1] A simple situation of this nature registers itself without explanation against the character of negroes in the records of the firms. The Pfister-Vogel Company had a house on Clinton Street in which lived twenty or more negroes. This location is eight or ten miles away from the community in which negroes live. There are no amusements for these young men around Clinton Street. The cars stop running at a comparatively early

which require immediate attention. But even these will not become alarming, if checked now, when preventive measures can be made practicable, attractive and easy.

The neighborhoods in which negroes live have long showed evidence of physical and moral deterioration. The addition of 1,400 negroes from the South, over 70 per cent of whom were brought to the city by companies seeking labor, hastened the deterioration and gave rise to problems where only tendencies existed before. Neighborhood life is conspicuously lax and the spirit of the community quite naturally comports with the looseness and immorality of the district. Though such conditions are plainly evident, no organized influence has been projected to correct them. As with the neighborhood, so with housing, crime, delinquency, education, recreation, industry, and the like, the conditions which retard developmental habits must have constant vigilance and treatment.

hour. If they go to the city they must either come back in a taxicab or spend the evening away from home. It is less expensive to spend the evening away. As a result they are late for work and may not report. If they report, they are tired and unfit for work. If they do not they are put down as irregular and unsteady.—Johnson, *Report on the Migration to Chicago.*

CHAPTER XI

The Situation at Points in the Middle West

The most important city in this section to be affected by the migration was Pittsburgh, the gateway to the West. The Pittsburgh district is the center of the steel industry. For this reason, the war caused the demand for labor to be extremely heavy there. Pittsburgh was one of the centers to which the greatest number of negroes went. Before the migration, a considerable number of negroes were employed there. In 1900, the negro population of Allegheny county, in which Pittsburgh is situated, was 27,753. In 1910 it was 34,217. When the migration began, the county had about 38,000 negroes. Investigations and estimates indicate that, at the end of 1917, the negro population of the county had increased to almost 66,000. Epstein in his survey of *The Negro Migrant in Pittsburgh* said: [1]

From a canvass of twenty typical industries in the Pittsburgh district, it was found that there were 2,550 negroes employed in 1915, and 8,325 in 1917, an increase of 5,775 or 227 per cent. It was impossible to obtain labor data from more than approximately sixty per cent of the negro employing concerns, but it is fair to assume that the same ratio of increase holds true of the remaining forty per cent. On this basis the number of negroes now employed in the district may be placed at 14,000. This means that there are about 9,750 more negroes working in the district today than there were in 1915, an addition due to the migration from the South.

According to Epstein, the migration had been going on for little longer than one year. Ninety-three per cent of those who gave the time of residence in Pittsburgh had been there less than one year. More than eighty per cent of the single men interviewed had been there less than six months. In the number who had been there for the longest period, married men predominated, showing the tendency of this class to become

[1] Epstein, *The Negro Migrant in Pittsburgh*, p. 7.

permanent residents. This fact becoming evident, some industrial concerns bringing men from the South, having learned from bitter experience that the mere delivery of negroes from a southern city did not guarantee a sufficient supply of labor, made an effort to secure married men only, and even to investigate them prior to their coming. Differences in recruiting methods may also explain why some employers and labor agents hold a very optimistic view of the negro as a worker, while others despair of him. The reason why Pittsburgh has been unable to secure a stable labor force is doubtless realized by the local manufacturers. Married negroes come to the North to stay. They desire to have their families with them, and if they are not accompanied North by their wives and children they plan to have them follow at the earliest possible date.

It would appear that the stability of the labor supply depended to a very large extent upon the housing conditions. It was found that in many instances men who had families went to other cities where they hoped to find better accommodations. The Pittsburgh manufacturer will never keep an efficient labor supply of negroes until he learns to compete with the employers of other cities in a housing program as well as in wages. The negro migration in Pittsburgh, however, did not cause a displacement of white laborers. Every man was needed, as there were more jobs than men to fill them. Pittsburgh's industrial life was for a time dependent upon the negro labor supply, and the city has not received a sufficient supply of negroes, and certainly not so many as smaller industrial towns, although the railroads and a few of the industrial concerns of the locality have had labor agents in the South. Yet, in spite of the difficulties because of the obstructive tactics adopted in certain southern communities to prevent the negro exodus, they have nevertheless succeeded in bringing several thousand negroes into this district. " One company, for instance," says Epstein, " which imported about a thousand men within the past year, had only about three hundred of these working at the time of the investigator's visit in July, 1917. One railroad, which is said to have brought about fourteen thousand people to the

North within the last twelve months, has been able to keep an average of only eighteen hundred at work." These companies, however, have failed to hold the newcomers.

The problems created by this sudden increase of Pittsburgh's population were very grave. In the early part of 1917, plans were formulated to make a social survey of the migrants in Pittsburgh. Cooperating in this survey were the University of Pittsburgh, the Associated Charities, the Social Service Commission of the Churches of Christ and the National League on Urban Conditions among Negroes. In March, 1917, the director of the Department of Public Health, instructed the sanitary inspectors to pay special attention to all premises occupied by the "newcomers." Another step in this direction was the establishment in that city of a branch of the National League on Urban Conditions among Negroes.

A survey made in 1917 showed that the housing situation was the most serious aspect of the migrants' social problems, and that in order to have improvements in other lines housing conditions must be made better. Because of the high cost of materials and labor incident to the war, because the taxation system still does not encourage improvements and because of investment attractions other than in realty, few houses had been built and practically no improvements had been made. This was most strikingly apparent in the poorer sections of the city. In the negro sections, for instance, there had been almost no houses added and few vacated by whites within the previous two years. The addition, therefore, of thousands of negroes just arrived from southern States meant not only the creation of new negro quarters and the dispersion of negroes throughout the city, but also the utmost utilization of every place in the negro sections capable of being transformed into habitations. Attics and cellars, storerooms and basements, churches, sheds and warehouses had to be employed for the accommodation of these newcomers. Whenever a negro had space which he could possibly spare, it was converted into a sleeping place; as many beds as possible were crowded into it, and the maximum number of men per bed were lodged. Either because their own rents were high or because they were unable to withstand the temptation of the sudden, and, for all they knew, temporary harvest, or perhaps because of the altruistic desire to assist their race fellows, a majority of the negroes in Pittsburgh converted their homes into lodging houses.

Because rooms were hard to come by the lodgers were not disposed to complain about the living conditions or the prices charged. They were only too glad to secure a place where they could share a half or at least a part of an unclaimed bed. It was no easy task to find room for a family, as most boarding houses would accept only single men, and refused to admit women and children. Many a man, who with his family occupied only one or two rooms, made place for a friend or former townsman and his family. In many instances this was done from unselfish motives and in a humane spirit.[1]

How the negroes are employed will throw more light on their situation. The Epstein investigation showed that

Ninety-five per cent of the migrants who stated their occupations were doing unskilled labor, in the steel mills, the building trades, on the railroads, or acting as servants, porters, janitors, cooks and cleaners. Only twenty, or four per cent out of 493 migrants whose occupations were ascertained, were doing what may be called semiskilled or skilled work, as puddlers, mold-setters, painters and carpenters. On the other hand, in the South 59 out of 529 claimed to have been engaged in skilled labor, while a large number were rural workers.

The following table shows the occupations of migrants in Pittsburgh as compared with statements of occupations in the South:

Occupations	In Pittsburgh	%	In South	%
Common laborer	468	95	286	54
Skilled or semiskilled	20	4	59	11
Farmer			81	15
Miner			36	7
Sawmill workers			9	2
Ran own farm or father's farm			22	5
Ran farm on crop sharing basis			33	6
Other occupations	5	1	0	0

It seems clear that most of the migrants were engaged in unskilled labor. The reason given by the manufacturers in

[1] Epstein, *The Negro Migrant in Pittsburgh,* pp. 7-8.

accounting for this disparity were that the migrants are ineffi-
cient and unstable, and that the opposition to them on the part
of the white labor prohibits their use on skilled jobs.[1] Ninety-
five per cent of the negro workers in the steel mills were unskilled
laborers. " In the bigger plants," says the investigator, " where
many hundreds of negroes are employed, almost one hundred
per cent are doing common labor, while in the smaller plants,
a few might be found doing labor which required some skill."
Epstein believes that this idea is often due to the prejudice of
the heads of departments and other labor employers. A sympathetic superintendent of one of the large steel plants said
that in many instances it was the superintendents and managers
themselves who are not alive to their own advantage, and so
oppose the negroes in doing the better classes of work. The
same superintendent said that he had employed negroes for
many years; that a number of them had been connected with
his company for several years; that they are just as efficient
as the white people. More than half of the twenty-five negroes
in his plant were doing semiskilled and even skilled work. He
had one or two negro foremen over negro gangs, and cited
an instance of a black man drawing $114 in his last two weeks'
pay. This claim was supported by a very intelligent negro who
was stopped a few blocks away from the plant and questioned
as to the conditions there. While admitting everything that
the superintendent said, and stating that there is now absolute
free opportunity for negroes in that plant, the man asserted
that these conditions have obtained within the last year.[2]

It was found that in the Pittsburgh district the great mass
of workers get higher wages than in the places from which

[1] The latter objection is illustrated by the case of the white bargemen of
a big steel company who wanted to walk out because black workers were
introduced among them, and who were only appeased by the provision of
separate quarters for the negroes. While there is an undeniable hostility
to negroes on the part of a few white workers, the objection is frequently
exaggerated by prejudiced gang bosses.

[2] The same superintendent told of an episode illustrating the amicable
relations existing in his shop between white and black workers. He related
that a gang of workers had come to him with certain complaints and the
threat of a walkout. When their grievances had been satisfactorily adjusted,
hey pointed to the lonely black man in their group and said that they were
t ready to go back unless their negro fellow worker was satisfied.

they come. Fifty-six per cent received less than $2 a day in the South, while only five per cent received such wages in Pittsburgh. However, the number of those who said they received high wages in the South is greater than the number of those receiving them there. Fifteen per cent said they received more than $3.60 a day at home, while only five per cent said they received more than that rate for twelve hours' work there. Sixty-seven per cent of the 453 persons stating their earnings here, earn less than $3 a day. Twenty-eight per cent earn from $3 to $3.60 a day, while only five per cent earn more than $3.60 a day. The average working day for both Pittsburgh and the South is ten and four-tenths hours. The average wage is $2.85 here; in the South it amounted to $2.15. It may be interesting to point out that the number of married men who work longer hours and receive more money is proportionately greater than that of the single men, who have not " given hostage to fortune."

Judging from what has been said about the habits of living among the negro migrants in Pittsburgh, they are of the best class of their race. Chief among those to be mentioned is their tendency to abstain from the use of intoxicants although it has often been said that the cause of the migration from the South was due to the desire of negroes in prohibition States to go where they may make free use of whisky. In this city it was observed that out of 470 persons who answered questions with reference to whether or not they imbibed only 210 of them said that they drank, while 267 made no use of intoxicants at all. It was also observed that among those who have families, the percentage of those addicted to drink is much smaller than that of others who are single or left their families in the South. This, no doubt, accounts for the orderly conduct of these negroes who, according to statistics, have not experienced a wave of crime. The records of the courts show numerous small offenses charged to the account of negroes, but these usually result from temptations and snares set by institutions of vice which are winked at by the community.

These negroes, on the whole, are thrifty and will eventually attach themselves permanently to the community through the acquisition of desirable property and elevation to positions of trust in the industries where they are employed. Evidences of the lazy and shiftless and the immoral are not frequent, because of a sort of spirit of thrift pervading the whole group. Many of the families have savings accounts in banks, and practically all of the married men separated from their families in the South send a large portion of their earnings from time to time. Money order receipts and stubs of checks examined show that these remittances to distant families range from between $5 to $10 a week. Others have seen fit to divert their income to objects more enterprising. They are educating their children, purchasing homes and establishing businesses to minister to the needs of their own peculiar group.

In view of the desirability of most migrants in this city, several persons have seen fit to make a comparison of the negro and foreign labor, with a view to determining whether or not the employment of negroes in the North will be permanent, as they may easily be displaced by the foreigners immigrating into this country in the future. The consensus of opinion is that the blacks are profitable laborers, but that their efficiency must be decidedly increased to compete with that of the white workers. Some of the faults observed are that they are as yet unadapted to the " heavy and pace-set labor in the steel mills." Accustomed to the comparatively easy going plantation and farm work of the South, it will take some time for these migrants to find themselves. " They can not even be persuaded to wait until pay day, and they like to get money in advance, following the habit that they acquired from the southern credit system. It is often secured on very flimsy pretexts and spent immediately in the saloons and similar places." Yet the very persons who make this estimate of the negro laborer say that the negroes born in the North or who have been in the North some time are as efficient as the whites, and that because of their knowledge of the language and the ways of this country, they are often much better than the foreign laborers who understand neither.

The principal industrial centers in Ohio to which the migrants went were Cincinnati, Middletown, Akron, Dayton, Springfield, Youngstown, Columbus and Cleveland. The city which took the lead in endeavoring to handle the migration problem was Cleveland. This was due to a considerable extent to the fact that the housing conditions in Cleveland were especially bad. Investigations made in the summer of 1917 by the Chamber of Commerce showed that housing conditions never were so in need of remedying as they were at that time. The influx of negroes, thousands of whom were living in box cars on railway sidings, was only one feature of the problem, investigators say. In nearly every part of the city, and especially in the vicinity of large manufacturing plants, workers are herded together, paying as much as $8 a week for a single room for a whole family.[1]

The Cleveland Welfare Federation appointed a committee composed of representatives of both races, to study problems made acute in Cleveland by the recent incoming of probably 10,000 negroes from the South. At the first meeting of this committee, August 3, 1917, the city welfare department announced that 61 per cent of the men in the workhouse at Warrensville were negroes and that of 100 women 66 were negroes. The normal proportion of negroes in the workhouse before the migration began was about 10 per cent, he said. This had mounted rapidly in the last year. It was brought out that the cause of this increase lay in housing congestion, lack of opportunities for recreation and because negro migrants are ignorant of the city's customs, laws and ordinances. A subcommittee was therefore appointed to look into this matter, as well as into that of perils surrounding newly arrived negro girls. A subcommittee was also appointed to study housing congestion and health problems. The secretary of the Cleveland Real Estate Board reiterated that there were 10,000 houses, renting at $25 and under, needed at the present time for both negro and white residents, and that, owing to labor difficulties and the high price of building materials, very little had been done to relieve the situation. He stated that a partial solution

[1] *Cleveland News,* August 11, 1917.

could be found in inducing both negro and white people who could afford to build or buy houses to do so, and thus free more houses for those who can not afford to buy them. It was asserted that unless something should be done before cold weather the housing problem would become acute.[1] To assist in meeting the house shortage a group of prominent negroes organized " The Realty Housing and Investment Company." [2]

The negro churches and other organizations cooperated in the effort to solve the problem of caring for the newly arrived negroes. In December, 1917, all the organizations and agencies working to aid the migrants were united in the Negro Welfare Association of Cleveland.[3] William R. Connors, a negro social worker, was employed as executive secretary of the new organization, beginning January 1, and offices were opened in the Phyllis Wheatley Association Building at East 40th Street and Central Avenue. The budget for the first year was estimated at about $5,000.

The organization acted as a clearing house for all the problems confronting the negro people there and cooperated with other agencies in the following activities: relief work, nursing service, legal aid, employment, promoting thrift, providing recreation through the public schools and otherwise, studying the delinquency problem, caring for discharged prisoners in cooperation with the workhouse and promoting community singing. It investigated the social conditions among negroes, with a view to establishing those agencies which are needed, or to point out the needs to the organization already established. It endeavored to educate the negro public to a full appreciation of the possi-

[1] *Cleveland Plain Dealer,* August 4, 1917.
[2] An advertisement of this company in the *Cleveland Advocate* was as follows:

Cleveland is short 10,000 houses:
The city on Lake Erie is face to face with the problem of *"Housing the People!"* We have been on the job day in and day out and are pleased to announce that *we have just played a master stroke.*
You may ask what is it? We will answer.
We have just secured the group of seven apartment houses which are rapidly nearing completion on East 40th Street between Central and Scoville Avenues. Three and four room suites with bath, hot water, electric lights, gas ranges, heating appliances, refrigerators, Murphy in-a-dor beds. Laundry just waiting to be occupied. All for colored people.
[3] *Cleveland Town Topics,* December 22, 1917.

bilities of a definite social program and to its responsibility for seeing that it is carried out.

In June, 1916, a call was issued for a statewide conference of representative white and colored people to be held at the capital of the State, Columbus, on July 12, 1916, to take steps toward caring for the 100,000 negro migrants believed to have remained in Ohio. Among those who signed the call were J. Walter Wills, President of Cleveland Association of Colored Men; Reverend H. C. Bailey, President of National Association for the Advancement of Colored People; W. S. Scarborough, President of Wilberforce University; Charles Johnson, Superintendent of Champion Chemical Company, Springfield, and Edward T. Banks, member of Charter Commission, Dayton.[1] The mayors of Ohio cities named delegates to the conference. At this conference the Ohio Federation for the Uplift of the Colored People was formed, and an extensive program designed to improve economic and social conditions was outlined. Branches of the Federation were soon established at Akron, Columbus, Cleveland, Cincinnati, Dayton, Piqua, Steubenville, Youngstown and other points.

Reports showing labor, housing, general welfare and health conditions among the negroes throughout the State were compiled and distributed broadcast. It was also decided to send lecturers through Ohio cities to visit negro centers for the purpose of instilling within the race a desire for better living conditions. A campaign was waged also to bring about greater censorship of motion pictures. Efforts were made to have the State Council of National Defense and the State and City Labor Bureaus actively interest themselves in the problem of negro employment.[2]

The State of Ohio also undertook an investigation of the migration movement. Reports to the Ohio branch, Council of National Defense, indicated a very serious situation resulting from the exodus of negroes. An investigation at direction of Governor Cox was conducted by the Council and State Depart-

[1] *Dayton News*, July 7, 1917.
[2] *Cincinnati Enquirer*, September 12, 1917

ment, to get as much information as possible concerning the unprecedented migration. The first work was a study of health conditions in several cities by the State Department of Health, which took immediate steps to correct evils. The negroes who were coming into the State were being crowded into the negro sections of the various cities in such a way that the health of these communities in many cases was being seriously threatened. The Council of National Defense asked the Ohio branch for information on the migration, particularly to learn if it had been artificially stimulated and accelerated by agencies that have paid so many dollars a head for every negro from the South.[1]

Detroit, because of its importance as an industrial center, was one of the places to which the largest number of migrants to Michigan went. The negro population of the city in 1910 was 5,741. It is now estimated that the city has between 25,000 and 35,000 blacks, three-fourths or more of whom have come there during the past two years. As elsewhere, the majority of the negroes are in unskilled occupations. There is, however, a considerable number of skilled and semiskilled workers. Detroit was formerly a city where the negro was restricted to a very few lines of work.

The wartime pressing needs of the industrial enterprises have caused the barriers to be removed. The available evidence that Detroit has removed the barriers from the employment of negroes in many lines is considerable. There were calls for 336 truckers, 160 molders, 109 machinists, 45 core makers and for a number of other miscellaneous skilled and semiskilled men. Most of the women were wanted in domestic and personal service in private homes, but 32 calls came from a garment factory, 18 from a cigar factory and 19 for ushers in a theater.

Their wages were exceptionally high according to Dr. George E. Haynes' intensive study of the returns of 407 families. One received between $30 and $39 a month; three received between $40 and $49, six received between $60 and $69; 20 received between $70 and $79; 96 received between $80 and $89; 6 received between $90 and $99; 27 received between $100 and $119;

[1] *Columbus Dispatch*, August 1, 1917.

21 received between $120 and $129, and 4 received $140 or more a month. There was a man working at $6.30 a day. The number of days they were employed a month could not be ascertained. There were 161 men whose monthly wages were doubtful or unknown, two men were the owners of a business and five were unemployed. Of the 45 women who were the heads of families, 13 were doing day's work at $2 a day and one at $2.50 a day, but the number of days they were employed could not be ascertained and so the monthly wages could not be calculated. There were two women earning between $40 and $49 a month and three earning between $70 and $79 a month. The monthly wages of 26 were doubtful or unknown. " As far as these figures are typical of the wages of negro workmen in Detroit," says Dr. Haynes, " they show that the prevailing wages of the men are from about $70 to $119 a month; for, 159 of the 194 men whose wages were ascertained were receiving wages ranging between these amounts. The prevailing wage for women is about that of those doing day work, $2 a day." [1]

In Detroit, as in other places, there is conflict of opinion as to the value of the negro as a laborer. The survey of the migrants there showed that there were diverse views about the suitability of negro labor. Mr. Charles M. Culver, General Manager of the Detroit Employers Association, thought some employers were highly pleased with negro workmen and some were not. He said:

There are two lines of adverse opinion about the negro as a workman; first, nine-tenths of the complaints of employers are that he is too slow. He does not make the speed that the routine of efficient industry demands. He is lacking in the regularity demanded by routine of industry day by day. Second, the negro has been observed to be disinclined to work out-of-doors when the cold weather comes. Employers have discussed this and have not found the negro satisfactory on this point. Unless the negroes overcome this practice employers will turn to other sources of supply when their present extreme needs are past. Employers must have a labor supply upon which they can depend at all seasons—laborers who will work out-of-doors winter as well as summer.

[1] Haynes, *Survey of the Migrants in Detroit.*

Speaking of the colored women employed in the manufacture of garments by the Krolick Company, Mr. Cohen, the superintendent, said his greatest difficulty was in overcoming the timidity of the girls and in inducing them to believe they can become successful operators and earn good wages.

The peculiar situation caused by the sudden increase of the city's negro population was met by organized efforts directed, in the main, by the local branch of the National League on Urban Conditions among Negroes, which here also took the lead in helping the migrants adjust themselves.[1]   Among the important things done by the league were the establishing of a vocational bureau, a bureau of investigation and information regarding houses, and a committee on recreation; the inaugurating of a ten cent " newcomers " community dance, which was held every Tuesday evening in a public school in the heart of the negro district; the development of athletic features for the immigrants, and the organization of a branch of " Camp Fire Girls."   The league induced one of the largest foundries to build low-priced homes for its negro employes near the plant. It also somewhat relieved the housing problem by the purchase of leases from the proprietresses of a number of disorderly houses which were closed by the police.   In each case the league persuaded some manufacturer to take over the lease, and in this way a large number of negro families were accommodated.   It also kept a list of vacant houses and was surprised to find how many of them were not listed by commercial real estate agents.

The league persuaded the police commissioner to appoint a special officer, selected by the league especially for the newcomers.   It is his duty to mingle with crowds on the streets where the newcomers congregate and urge them not to make a nuisance of themselves by blocking sidewalks, boisterous be-

[1] The Urban League is maintained by the Associated Charities and private individuals to study Detroit's negro problem and improve the condition of the city's negroes.   Forrester B. Washington is director in charge of the league.   The organization will aim to direct negro sentiment and support along lines of best interests for Detroit.—*Detroit News*, November 6, 1916.

havior and the like. He was also provided with cards direct-
ing newcomers to the office of the league when in need of employment. The league itself kept a close watch on the negro
underworld of Detroit and immediately apprised the police when
dives were developed especially to prey on the immigrant.

The Board of Commerce cooperated in a movement for the
investigation and improvement of working conditions of negro
employes in the various manufacturing plants in Detroit. The
Board of Health gave considerable assistance in obtaining better
and more sanitary housing conditions. The aid of several
mothers' clubs among the colored women was enlisted to instruct
immigrant mothers in the proper diet and clothing for children
in a northern climate. From the outset, the aim was not only
to put each migrant in a decent home but also to connect him
with some church. Many times the churches reciprocated with
considerable material as well as spiritual assistance.

Valued cooperation was given by the Young Negroes' Progressive Association, a body of thirty-four young colored men,
most of whom attended the various schools and colleges about
Detroit. They have been the finest possible agents in the development of all the different activities. In the adjustment
of the negro, a definite place must be given to the development
of industrial efficiency. In pursuance of this object the league,
with the assistance of the Progressive Association, carried on
a movement.[1] Representatives of the two organizations visit
the various factories where large numbers of negroes are employed and talk to them during the noon hour on the necessity
of creating the best possible impression at the present time so

---

[1] Two surveys of the migrants in Detroit were made. One was under the
auspices of the negro committee of the Home Missions' Council of the
Churches of Christ in America and was published under the title, " Negro
Newcomers in Detroit." This survey investigated industrial opportunities,
housing and recreation facilities, and the work which the churches were
doing and should do for Detroit's newcomers.

The Church Extension Committee of the Detroit Presbytery made a survey
of the negro problem in Detroit. This survey showed that the negro population of the city has grown from 5,000 in 1910 to 21,000 in 1917. The negro
churches of the city are utterly inadequate to take care of the religious needs
of the race here, it was shown.

that they may be certain of retaining their jobs in the future. At the same time, the speakers circulate these cards:

WHY HE FAILED

He watched the clock.
He was always behindhand.
He asked too many questions.
He wasn't ready for the next step.
He did not put his heart in his work.
He learned nothing from his blunders.
He was contented to be a second-rater.
He didn't learn that the best part of his salary was not in his pay envelope.

—Success.

CHAPTER XII

The Situation at Points in the East

No less conspicuous as attractions to the negroes of the South were the various industries of the State of Pennsylvania. Although not so closely connected with the Black Belt of the South as are so many of the industrial centers of the West, Pennsylvania nevertheless was sought by many of these migrants because of the long accepted theory that this commonwealth maintains a favorable attitude toward persons of color. It drew upon this population too because of the very urgent need for workers in its numerous industries during the labor crisis resulting from the falling off of the foreign immigration. When, moreover, manufacturing establishments of the State multiplied as elsewhere because of the demand for the manufacture of munitions of war, this need became more urgent than ever.

According to the census of 1910, the State of Pennsylvania had 193,919 inhabitants of negro blood, 84,459 of whom lived in the city of Philadelphia. During the recent rush to that commonwealth, however, investigators are now of the opinion that the negro population of that State is hardly less than 300,000. These migrants were, of course, not all settled in the city of Philadelphia. Here we see another example of a rerouting point, a place where the migration broke bulk, scattering itself into the various industrial communities desiring labor. Among the other cities and towns receiving this population were practically all of those within a radius of about one hundred miles of Philadelphia, such as Lancaster, Pottsville, York, Altoona, Harrisburg and certain other towns lying without the State, as in the case of Wilmington, Delaware, a site of a large munitions plant. In some cases the negro population in these towns increased more than 100 per cent in a few days.

The chief factors in the bringing in of these negroes from the South were the leading railroads like the Erie and Pennsylvania. During the shortage of labor, these corporations found it impossible to keep their systems in repair. In this situation, they, like the smaller concerns further west, sent labor agents to the South to induce negroes to supply this demand. Unfortunately, however, so many of the negroes who had their transportation paid by these firms counted it more profitable to leave their employ immediately after arriving, because of the unusually high wages offered by smaller industries in just as urgent need of labor. Instead of supplying their own demand, therefore, the railroads were benefiting their neighbors.

A better idea as to the extent of the congestion made possible by this influx of newcomers may be obtained from the comments of observers in that section. Traveling men tell us of the crowded houses and congested streets which marked the places wherever these migrants stopped. Housing facilities being inadequate, temporary structures were quickly built and when these did not suffice, in the case of railroads, ordinary tents and box cars were used to shelter the new laborers. Owing to these unsatisfactory conditions and the inability of employers to ameliorate them, the migration was to some extent discouraged, and in a few cases a number of the migrants returned to their homes in the South, so that the number that actually came into the State is much less than it would have been, had it been possible to receive and adequately accommodate the negroes in their new homes.

In Philadelphia the situation at first became unusually critical. Being closer to the Southland than most of the large cities of the country, the people of Philadelphia are much more prejudiced against the negro than those in some other northern cities. It was necessary, therefore, upon their arrival in that city for them to crowd into the district largely restricted to negroes, giving rise to such unhappy conditions as to jeopardize the peace and health of the community. Numbers of these migrants died from exposure during the first winter, and others who died because of their inability to stand the northern climate made the situation seem unusually alarming. It was necessary, therefore, to organize social workers to minister to the peculiar needs of these newcomers. Appeals were made in their behalf and a number of prominent citizens felt that it was necessary to urge them to remain in the South.

The solution of this problem was rendered a little more difficult for the reason that here, as in many other centers in the North, the newcomers were not welcomed by their own race. Philadelphia had for years been pointed to as having a respectable, thrifty and prosperous colored population, enjoying the good will and the cooperation of the best white people in the community. These northern negroes felt then that the coming of their brethren in the rough did them a decided injury in giving rise to a race problem in a northern community where it had not before figured. This unusual influx of other members of the race greatly stimulated that tendency to segregate negro children in the schools, to the deep regret of the older citizens of Philadelphia. Other social privileges as in theaters, churches and the like, formerly allowed the negro citizens of that city, tended gradually to be withdrawn.

The negro migrants were not altogether innocent. Many of them used their liberty in their northern home as a stumbling block. Receiving there such high wages which they could not judiciously spend, the unwise of their group used this unusually large income to their own detriment and to that of the community. It was indeed difficult to restrain a poor man who never had had a few dollars, when just arrived from a section of the country where he had not only been poor but restricted even in expending what income he received. Many of them received $6, $7 and in a few cases $8 to $10 a day. They frequented saloons and dens of vice, thereby increasing the number of police court cases and greatly staining the record of the negroes in that city. A number of fracases, therefore, broke out from time to time, growing in intensity in keeping with the condition to which the community, unaccustomed to negro neighbors, saw fit to manifest its displeasure.

This finally culminated in the recent riots in Philadelphia in which a number of blacks and whites were killed.

Feeling that they did not have the support of the officers of the law, the negroes of the city organized a Colored Protective Association and raised a fund for the prosecution of policemen and others who might aid mobs. The method of strengthening itself is to organize the churches of the city with a view to securing the cooperation of every negro there. To advance this work, a large sum has been raised. Other efforts of this sort in behalf of the negroes in Philadelphia have been made by the National Association for the Advancement of Colored People and the Armstrong Association in cooperation with the National League on Urban Conditions among Negroes.

Social workers in general soon found it necessary to address themselves to the task of readjusting these migrants.[1] The Philadelphia Academy of Medicine, composed of negro physicians, dentists and druggists, put into effect measures calculated to meet requirements for housing, sanitation, medical attention and education. Systematic medical inspections were given, and projects for the erection of houses and the adaptation of existing buildings for lodgings are under way. Eighty negro physicians of the city collected information which took the form of a weekly report of the Bureau of Health. Real estate dealers were asked to submit lists of every house immediately available for the relief of the overcrowded buildings then occupied by the negroes and to provide hundreds of new ones, cheaply but substantially constructed. Stereopticon lectures and talks were given on an increasing scale in all the negro churches telling the new arrivals how to care for themselves in the Philadelphia climate, how to avoid colds, which lead to pneumonia and tuberculosis, the two most common diseases among them, and other useful information in general.

The Interdenominational Ministerial Union of Philadelphia, embracing all the negro ministers of the city, drew up certain resolutions setting forth their views relative to the migration and making some suggestions concerning the situation in Phila-

[1] The *Philadelphia North American,* February 2, 1917.

delphia. They pledged themselves to look after the comfort of the migrants in every way possible, urged them to join the churches and other organizations for improvement, and send their children to the schools, and to utilize the libraries, night schools and other agencies of culture which were denied them in the South. These ministers urged them also to work regularly, and give their best services to their employers regardless of pay, remembering always that the race is on trial in them; that they save their money, and purchase homes and become a part of the substantial citizenry as soon as possible.[1]

A Negro Migration Committee was formed, composed of eight workers from social agencies and charitable societies, to provide suitable housing for negro families arriving in this city and to aid them in getting work. Each member of the committee is to work through the organization he represents and be responsible for one specific phase of the problem.[2]

Notwithstanding the efforts that were made to improve the housing conditions, the situation in this respect continued to grow worse. In December of 1917, representatives of the various social agencies and of the corporations employing large numbers of negroes met in a conference on the housing situation. " All the questions involved in the reasons for the colored people coming north and the problem of housing and caring for them were seriously discussed."

Some representatives of the corporations asserted that the men were not reliable and dependable, going from place to place and only working a few days in each week. The social service workers stated that the reason for this is that there are not a sufficient number of houses in which to take care of the men and their families, and that the districts in which they lived were shamefully crowded. According to these workers the only way in which the men can be made satisfied is by providing more homes for them in sanitary and wholesome quarters. After thoroughly considering the problem a permanent committee was appointed to deal with the problem in all its aspects.[3]

One of the most effective agencies for dealing with the situation created by thousands of negroes migrating north was the

[1] Resolutions of the Interdenominational Union.
[2] *Philadelphia Inquirer*, March 2, 1917.
[3] *The Living Church*, December 22, 1917.

Armstrong Association. This association gave special attention to stabilizing negro labor and to improving the housing
conditions. The association brought before several corporations
conditions of housing and recreation which would enable them
to retain their workers. They provided a negro welfare worker
for the American International Shipbuilding Company, to attend
to the stabilizing of negro labor. The association is perfecting
plans for better housing of negro workers and the providing
of recreation centers, such as are now enjoyed in virtually every
city by the white workers. The association obtained the cooperation of a number of large industrial firms and corporations in
this city, to aid it in the employment of competent negro welfare
workers to help adjust existing conditions, making for greater
efficiency and reliability among the negro race.

The demand for labor by the many industrial plants located
in New Jersey caused that State to get a very large proportion
of the negro migrants and as a result to have, in acute form,
the problem of housing conditions and the other problems incident to a large number of migrants being within her borders.
To assist in caring for the situation a Negro Welfare League
was organized with branches at various points in the State.

Writing on the situation in New Jersey, a contributor of *The
Survey,* for February 17, 1917, states:

The native negro residents of the city and suburban towns have been kind
and generous in helping the southern stranger. They have collected money
to send numbers back home, and when the bitter cold weather began they
collected and distributed thousands of garments. Resident negroes have also
taken hundreds of newcomers into their own homes until rooms could be
found for them. But, while different churches and kind hearted people
had been most active in helping individually, there was no concerted movement to bring all these forces together until the organization of the Negro
Welfare League of New Jersey. Industries of New Jersey have utterly
failed to provide the housing which would enable their negro help to live
decently and in enough comfort so that while growing accustomed to their
unusual work, they might be stimulated to become useful and efficient.

In the last two weeks the Negro Welfare Committee, with the help of
an investigation of 120 self-supporting families, all of whom were found
in the worst sections of the city, showed that 166 adults—only twenty of
whom are over forty years of age—and 134 children, a total of 300 souls,
are all crowded into insanitary dark quarters, averaging four and two-

sevenths persons to a room. These fifty-three families paid a total rent per month of $415.50, an average of $7.66. The average wage of these people is $2.60 a day. In not one of the 120 families was there a wage earner making the maximum wage of $3 and $4 a day. Some of the reports in brief were: " Wife and children living over a stable. Husband earning $11 a week." Three families in four rooms, "a little house not fit for a chicken coop." " A sorry looking house for so much money, $15 a month; doors off the hinges, water in the cellar, two families in five rooms." " Indescribable; so dark they must keep the light burning all day." " This family lives in three rooms on the second floor of a rickety frame house, built on the side of a hill, so that the back rooms are just above the ground. The entrance is in a muddy, disorderly yard and is through a tunnel in the house. The rooms are hard to heat because of cracks. A. boy of eighteen was in bed breathing heavily, very ill with pneumonia, delirious at times." Unused to city life, crowded into dark rooms, their clothing and household utensils unsuitable, the stoves they have brought being all too small to heat even the tiny rooms they have procured (the instalment houses are charging from $20 to $30 for these stoves), shivering with the cold from which they do not know how to protect themselves, it is small wonder that illness has overtaken large numbers.[1]

Newark, New Jersey, was one of the places to which the migrants first came in large numbers. William H. Maxwell, President of the Negro Forward Movement, of that city, issued an appeal for the protection from the unscrupulous of southern negroes migrating to Newark. He declared that they were being made to work for lower wages than they had been promised and that storekeepers and dealers were charging them high prices for worthless goods. The Newark Presbytery took up the matter of proper housing and clothing of the migrants who were unaccustomed to the rigors of a northern climate.

On September 23, 1917, a State conference of negroes was held in Newark to devise ways and means to cooperate with the State authorities in looking after the welfare of migrants. Soon after this conference, it was decided to establish a State bureau, " for the welfare and employment of the colored citizens in the State and particularly to look after the housing, employment and education of the citizens migrating from the South." On October 12, Governor Edge had a number of social workers among the negroes to meet him, " to discuss the several perplexing and grave economic, industrial and social

[1] Cotton Pickers in Northern Cities, *The Survey*, February 17, 1917.

problems arising from the steady influx of the negro migrants from the South." The conference was held in the Assembly room at the State House. Col. Lewis T. Bryant, Commissioner of Labor, presided. After many reports and discussions of work accomplished in various parts of the State, the body voted to accept the proposed Negro Welfare Bureau, under the Department of Labor. A fund of $7,500 is available for the coming year's maintenance and work. The scope of this bureau's work was employment, housing, social welfare and readjustment, education and legal fairness. This bureau acted as a welfare clearing house for all social agencies working for the betterment of the colored people.

At the next session of the legislature, a bill was passed, February, 1918, establishing in the Department of Labor the Negro Welfare Employment Bureau. According to a report of the work of the Negro Welfare Bureau made public in April, 1918, considerable progress in the work of improving both the migrating negroes to New Jersey from the South as well as the members of the race generally who have been in this State for some time has been made. With the possible exception of Salem and Hudson counties, the sheriffs of the State report no increase of criminality from the migration of negroes from the South. At Pennsgrove in Salem county, where the Du Pont powder plants are located, Sheriff William T. Eiffin reports that considering the increase in population there has been an increase in crime in that county, but that the situation is well in hand and diminishing to normal.[1]

Hartford was one of the industrial centers to which large numbers of the migrating negroes went. The housing problem became acute and the chief efforts of those endeavoring to better the conditions of migrants was along this line. Religious, civic and commercial bodies gave attention to the amelioration of this problem.[2] The problem of housing negroes who were coming in greater numbers each year to Hartford was taken up briefly by speakers at the 128th annual meeting of the Hart-

[1] *The Courier* (Camden, N. J.), April 30, 1918.
[2] *The Hartford Courant,* September 19, 1917.

ford Baptist Association at the Shiloh Baptist Church. It was decided to bring the housing problem before the attention of the Chamber of Commerce, which, it was said, some time before had appointed a committee to investigate it. Negroes complained that they were obliged to pay higher rent than white folks and that they were obliged by landlords to live together in cramped quarters that were, by reason of the crowding, insanitary. They said also that the living of several families almost as one family leads to a breaking down of the moral and religious ideals.[1] Conditions in Hartford resulting from the bringing of more than 2,500 negroes from the South were discussed at the fall meeting of the Confidential Exchange with a view to preparing for these new arrivals.

At the June, 1917, meeting of the Chamber of Commerce, a committee was appointed from that body to investigate housing conditions and to cooperate with other agencies in improving them. The committee met frequently through the summer with the housing committee of the Civic Club, in an endeavor to ascertain the facts bearing upon the present situation. It had before it leading colored citizens, ministers, business men and industrial workers, some of whom have lived here for years and others who have recently arrived from the South. It was discovered that there was, at that time, plenty of work and at good wages, but the universal complaint was the lack of homes suitable for proper living and the extortionate prices asked for rents. Negroes in Hartford were suffering from the cupidity of landlords. They were obliged to live in poor tenements and under unhealthful conditions because accommodations of another class were withheld from them. For such inferior accommodations they were charged outrageous rents, because selfish property owners knowing that negroes must live charged all the traffic would bear. Partial relief was obtained from the immediate need by the purchase of buildings already erected, and homes for them were later built. It appeared that for the first time in many years Hartford had a race problem on its hands.

[1] The *Hartford Post,* October 9, 1917.

CHAPTER XIII

Remedies for Relief by National Organizations

The sudden influx of thousands of negro workers to northern industrial centers created and intensified problems. More comprehensive and definite plans for aiding the migrants were, therefore, worked out and more effective methods of help instituted during 1917. A conference on negro migration was held in New York City under the auspices of the National League on Urban Conditions among Negroes, January 29-31, 1918. Among those attending the conference were representatives of capital, of labor, of housing conditions, the Immigration Bureau of Social Uplift Work for Negroes and others. The subjects considered were causes and consequences of the migration, present conditions of those migrating and what is to be done to aid in the negroes' adjustment to their new environment.

The conference was of the impression that negroes, then migrating to the North in unprecedented numbers, were preparing to come in larger numbers in the spring. It, therefore, recommended that wherever possible, whether in the city or rural community, organizations be formed to foster good feeling between the two races, to study the health, school and work needs of the negro population, to develop agencies and stimulate activities to meet those needs, by training and health protection to increase the industrial efficiency of negroes and to encourage a fairer attitude toward negro labor, especially in regard to hours, conditions and regularity of work and standard of wages, and to increase the respect for law and the orderly administration of justice. It further recommended that similar organizations be formed or existing organizations urged to take action which, in addition to the purposes already mentioned, should seek to instruct the negro migrants as to the dress, habits and methods of living necessary to withstand the rigors of the northern climate; as to efficiency, regularity and application demanded of workers in the North; as to the danger of dealing or going with unscrupulous or vicious persons and of frequenting questionable resorts; as to the opportunities offered by the towns and cities of the North in schools, hospitals, police protection and employment, and as to facilities offered by the church, Y. M. C. A. and other organizations.

The various religious denominations among negroes were profoundly affected by the migration movement. The sudden moving of thousands of communicants from one section of the country to the other caused many churches in the South to become disorganized and in some instances to be broken up. In the North the facilities of particular denominations were inadequate to accommodate the new communicants who would worship in the church of their particular faith. In some instances, it was necessary to hold double services in order that all who wished to attend the services might be accommodated. A writer in the *Southwestern Christian Advocate,* the organ of the negro members of the Methodist Episcopal Church, said: " The movement of the negroes by the thousands from the South to the North raises a many sided question. The missionary view is the logical view for the church, and that side of the question falls logically upon her hands for solution." [1]

The Boards of Missions of white denominations carrying on work among negroes made studies of the migration movement. Dr. Gilbert N. Brink, Secretary for Education of the American Baptist Home Mission Society, issued a pamphlet on " Negro Migration, What does it Mean? " [2] " The Invasion from Dixie " was the title of a circular issued on the migration by the Board of Home Missions and Church Extension of the Methodist Episcopal Church. In this circular two questions were asked with reference to the migrants. " What are you going to do for them?" and " How may we best serve this

[1] *Southwestern Christian Advocate,* New Orleans, La.
[2] *Ibid.*

most pressing need of the present time?" The circular further said:

The problem as seen from the viewpoint of the Methodist Episcopal Church is twofold. First, somehow to conserve the work we have already done in the South where the migration is leaving. Second, to provide religious opportunities for those people who have come from our own churches of the South as well as those unreached by church influences, so that at the beginning of their new life in the North they may all have the influence of the Church of Jesus Christ to shape and mold their future.

The Home Missions Council, which is composed of representatives from the boards doing missionary work in the United States, through its committee on negro work had a survey made of the migrants in Detroit. The results of this survey were published under the title "Negro Newcomers in Detroit." Detroit was selected because of the large numbers of negroes, who had been attracted to that city, and also because it was believed that the conditions in Detroit, although changing, were sufficiently typical of other northern industrial centers as to give a fairly accurate understanding of this modern phase of the negro problem, which might have acute and serious aspects if not speedily cared for by an enlightened judgment, and the quickened conscience of the Christian church.

The African Methodist Episcopal Church through its annual conferences, its Bishops' Council and its Missionary Department, undertook to meet the migration situation as it affected and imposed duties on that denomination. The Bishops' Council recommended to all the departments of the church that, to meet the needs of the church as to the expenditure of money in the home field of the North and Northwest for the benefit of "our migrating people," that they should do the best they could, "in assisting in the establishment of missions and church houses for our beloved people, consistent with their obligations already provided for by law and by the action of the Missionary Board."[1] A circular containing the following questions was sent out to the A. M. E. churches throughout the North.

[1] Report of Bishop's Council, A.M.E. Church, 1917.

How many persons, to your knowledge, have come from the South into your vicinity during the past year?

In what sections of your city are they located?

To what extent are they African Methodists?

From what section of the South have they come?

What reasons do they give for coming to the North?

To what extent have they found employment? At what, and what is the average wage paid?

Have you a Lookout Committee in your church to seek these people? If not, what organized effort is being put forth to church them?

Has any special mission work been started among or for our southern brethren, in your vicinity? If so, what and where?

What number of people from the South have united with your church during the past year?

How do they affiliate with your people?

What is the attitude of your members toward them?

So far as you have seen, is the better plan, where the numbers warrant it, to establish a distinct mission for them or bring them into the already established churches?

Bishop R. A. Carter, of the Colored Methodist Episcopal Church, after an extended trip north in the interest of the work of his denomination for the migrants, published in the official organ of his church a description of the situation as he found it, and what the Colored Methodist Episcopal Church should do to assist in meeting the needs of the situation. He said:

I have just returned from an extended trip through the great Northwest, having visited St. Louis, Chicago, Gary, Milwaukee, Detroit, Cleveland, Pittsburgh, Clarksburg and West Virginia . . . Heretofore the few church houses in those cities have been sufficient for the colored people who were there. Since the migration of our people in such great numbers, the church facilities are alarmingly inadequate. It is necessary to hold two services at the same time in many churches and then hundreds are turned away for lack of room. It is pathetic to have to tell people who attend one service not to return to the next so that a new crowd may be accommodated. Yet that is just what must be done in many instances up that way now. There must be more churches established in all the large cities of the North and East and Northwest for our people or serious results will obtain in the future.

He considered the opportunity and duty of the C. M. E. Church as great and urgent. He recommended the purchase of vacant white churches offered for sale and the transfer of some of the best pastors. He urged that there be launched a movement for a great centenary rally for $500,000 with which to take advantage of the great opportunity which confronted the race in the North.

Before the migration movement the strength of the negroes in labor unions was largely in the South. In this section they were found in considerable numbers in the carpenters, bricklayers, plasterers, longshoremen and miners unions. In the North, however, they were not generally connected with the unions mainly for the reason that, excepting the hod carriers, teamsters, asphalt and cement workers and a few other organizations of unskilled laborers, they were not found in any occupation in sufficient numbers to necessitate being seriously considered by organized labor. The necessities of the industrial situation created by the war, however, brought thousands of negroes north and into trades and occupations in which hitherto they had not been found at all or only in negligible numbers. A change in attitude, therefore, was necessary. At the 1910 annual meeting of the National Council of the American Federation of Labor a resolution was unanimously passed inviting negroes and all other races into the Labor Federation. The officers of the Federation were instructed to take measures to see that negro workmen as well as workmen of other races be brought into the union. In 1913 this action was reaffirmed with the assertion that

Many years ago the American Federation of Labor declared for the thorough organization of all working people without regard to sex, religion, race, politics or nationality; that many organizations affiliated with the American Federation of Labor have within their membership negro workmen with all other workers of their trade, and the American Federation of Labor has made and is making every effort within its power for the organization of these workmen.[1]

At its 1916 annual convention held in November at Baltimore, the American Federation of Labor considered the question of negro migration. The question was brought formally

[1] Report of Proceedings, American Federation of Labor, annual session, 1913.

before the convention by the Ohio State Federation of Labor and the Cleveland Federation of Labor reciting that: "The investigation of such emigration and impo tation of negroes in the State of Ohio had demonstrated to the satisfaction of labor leaders in that State that they were being brought north for the purpose of filling the places of union men demanding better conditions, as in the case of freight handlers." Believing that "the conditions that prevailed in Ohio might apply in all northern States," the president and Executive Council of the Federation were instructed to begin a movement looking towards the organization of negroes in the southern States." [1]

At the 1917 convention of the American Federation of Labor held at Buffalo, New York, the question of negro labor was again considered. It was observed that the colored laborers and helpers throughout the southeastern district were not as familiar with the labor movement as they should be, especially upon the different railroads of the southeastern territory; and that there were fifteen different railroads in the district for which there were only four colored locals. Feeling that a negro organizer, because of his racial and social relations among his people, could accomplish much in organizing the forces into unions, the National Convention appointed a negro railroad man as organizer for the territory as above mentioned. Another set of resolutions, relating to the general condition of negroes in the United States, making suggestions to secure the cooperation of the American people and the national government in an endeavor to have the nations participating in the coming world peace conference agree upon a plan to turn over the African continent or parts thereof to the African race and those descendants of said race who live in America and desire to return to Africa, and thus enable the black race to work out its own destiny on an equality with other peoples of the earth, was referred to a committee. The report was, "Your committee can not be responsible for and rejects the statements contained in the resolution, but, inasmuch as por-

[1] Report of Proceedings, American Federation of Labor, annual session, 1916.

tions of it refer to the organization of negro workers, the committee recommends that that portion be referred to the Executive Council." [1]

At the annual meeting of the National League on Urban Conditions among Negroes, held in New York City, January 29-31, 1918, resolutions relating to labor unions and the negroes were adopted and a committee was appointed to place the resolutions before the executive committee of the American Federation of Labor. The resolutions adopted were as follows:

For the first time in the history of America, the negro working man is in large numbers getting a chance to offer his service at a fair wage for various kinds of work for which he is fitted. This opportunity, however, has come as a result of conditions over which neither he, nor those offering him the chance, have control.

In the city of New York, on the 31st day of January, 1918, we in conference assembled under the auspices of the National League on Urban Conditions among Negroes, while in no way seeking to condone the existence of the worldwide war which has been forced upon our beloved country, wish to express our gratitude for the industrial changes wrought and to record our prayer that the benefits thus far derived by the negro may continue and so enlarge as to embrace full and fair opportunity in all the walks of life.

I. We wish especially to address ourselves to the American Federation of Labor which at its recent convention in Buffalo, New York, voiced sound democratic principles in its attitude toward negro labor.

We would ask the American Federation of Labor, in organizing negroes in the various trades, to include: (1) skilled as well as unskilled workmen, (2) northern as well as southern workmen, (3) government as well as civilian employes, (4) women as well as men workers.

We would have negro labor handled by the American Federation of Labor in the same manner as white labor; (1) when workmen are returning to work after a successful strike; (2) when shops are declared "open" or "closed"; (3) when union workers apply for jobs.

We would have these assurances pledged not with word only, but by deeds—pledged by an increasing number of examples of groups of negro workmen given a "square deal."

With these accomplished, we pledge ourselves to urge negro working men to seek the advantages of sympathetic cooperation and understanding between men who work.

II. We would also address ourselves to the Labor Bureau of the United States Government.

In our national effort to speed up production of articles essential to the

[1] Report of Proceedings, American Federation of Labor, annual session, 1917.

conduct of the war as well as the production of other goods, let us not lose sight of our duty to our country in quantity production by an unreasonable prejudice in many quarters against the use of negro labor. Negro workmen are loyal and patriotic, cheerful and versatile. In some sections there is an oversupply of such labor; in other sections a shortage.

We would urge the appointment of one or two competent negroes in the Department of Labor to serve as assistants in each of the bureaus in distributing negro labor to meet war and peace needs.

III. We would urge negro workmen to remain cheerful and hopeful in work; to be persevering in their efforts to improve in regularity, punctuality and efficiency, and to be quick to grasp all opportunities for training both themselves and their children. Success lies in these directions.

IV. We would impress upon employers the fact that the efficiency of their employes during work hours depends very largely on the use made of the non-working hours. Most of the complaints against negro labor can be removed if proper housing, decent amusement, fair wages and proper treatment are provided.[1]

These resolutions were presented to the executive officers of the American Federation of Labor on February 12, 1918, by a committee composed of E. K. Jones, Director of National League on Urban Conditions among Negroes, Robert R. Moton, Principal of Tuskegee Institute, Archibald H. Grimke, Thomas Jesse Jones, specialist in the United States Bureau of Education, J. R. Shillady, Secretary of the National Association for the Advancement of Colored People, Fred R. Moore, editor of the *New York Age,* George W. Harris, editor of the *New York News,* and Emmett J. Scott, special assistant to the Secretary of War. The committee requested of the Executive Council that a committee be appointed by the American Federation of Labor to confer with a committee representing the interests of the negroes. This request was granted.

At the American Federation of Labor annual convention held at St. Paul, Minnesota, in June, 1918, the problem of negro workers and organized labor again received considerable attention. B. S. Lancaster, a negro delegate to the convention from Mobile, Alabama, offered a resolution asking for the appointment of a negro to organize negroes not now affiliated with unions in the shipbuilding trades. Another resolution

[1] Minutes of Session, National League on Urban Conditions, January 29-31, 1918.

was to the effect that negro porters, cooks, waiters and wait-resses, section hands and all negro railway employes to be organized. The press reports of the convention under date of June 12, said:

Dr. R. R. Moton, Principal of the Tuskegee Institute, and J. R. Shillady, of the National Association for the Advancement of Colored People, are authors of a communication asking for closer cooperation between white and colored workers. They ask that Mr. Gompers prepare a statement on his stand toward negro labor, and charge that some unions discriminate against colored workers. They urge consideration of revision of union charters to permit negroes to become members. The communication was referred.[1]

These efforts were not without some result, for sentiment began to change. In its August, 1918, issue the editor of the *Labor News* of Detroit, Michigan, said:

The time has arrived for the American labor movement to face squarely the fact that the negro is a big factor in our industrial life, and that he must be taken into account in the adjustment of our economic differences. Never again can the negro be ignored. Time and time again the selfish masters of industry have used him to batter your organizations to pieces, and, in-stead of trying to win him over, you have savagely fought him, because they used him as a strikebreaker. But the negro must be made to see the value of organization to himself, and he must be incorporated into and made a part of the great labor movement. It is a stupid policy to try to keep him out. Let us work to shift him from his present unhappy position, where he is despised by the big business element, notwithstanding his utility as a strikebreaker, and hated by unionists for his loyalty to the open shop element. Unionism must welcome the negro to its ranks.

[1] Report of M. N. Work on migration to the North.

CHAPTER XIV

Public Opinion Regarding the Migration

It was to be expected that a movement which so profoundly affected the social and economic life of the South would be widely discussed, and that the resulting discussions, wherein were set forth at length the views of whites and negroes, would throw much light upon the conditions existing prior to the movement. How the South viewed this taking away of a large part of her labor supply was stated in letters to the newspapers and in newspaper editorials. There were two views as to the effect of the migration on the South. One view held that the movement would benefit the South in that the negro population would be more evenly distributed over the entire country and as a result the race problem would be more truly national. The other view was that negro labor was a necessity for the South, and the drawing of a considerable part of this labor north was seriously detrimental to the South's economic interests.

The following are examples of expressions by those holding the view that the migration would benefit the South:

The New Orleans *Times Picayune* said:

Despite the attitude of certain extreme papers of the North that there was a broad conspiracy existing here to prevent the negroes from leaving, the records show that many southern papers and people welcomed the movement, believing that it would have a beneficial effect on the South by removing the negro majorities in many districts and in at least two States, South Carolina and Mississippi. The problems of negro majorities is rapidly working itself out. Louisiana, a State in which the negro was more numerous a few decades ago, is white today by several hundred thousand, and will have a million more whites by the next census. South Carolina and Mississippi expect to report white majorities in the next ten years as they are drifting rapidly in that direction, and negro emigration will help this condition along.

During the first months of this negro movement northward, a number of South Carolina papers, led by the *Columbia State,* instead of expressing apprehension over these departures, showed satisfaction that the State was getting rid of its excess of negroes. At the Southern Commercial Congress in a session at Norfolk, Judge Francis D. Winston, of North Carolina, expressed this same view of the situation in a resolution which declares that: "The complete industrial, intellectual and social development of the southern States can be secured only when the negro becomes a part of the citizenship of our sister States, and that we will encourage all movements tending to an equitable distribution of our negro population among the other States of the Union.

It is not likely that there will be any serious objection to a declaration of this kind in favor of the more equitable distribution of the negroes throughout the country as the question involved can then be better handled. No encouragement to the negroes to leave the South will be held out, but there will be no effort made to keep the negroes from going beyond explaining the situation to them.[1]

A comment of the *Nashville Banner* was:

From a logical point of view that looks beyond immediate emergencies, the southern whites should encourage negro emigration to the North, not for the cynical motives that impelled the late Hon. Jeff Davis while Governor of Arkansas to pardon negro convicts on condition that they go to Massachusetts to live, but to relieve the South of the entire burden and all the brunt of the race problem, and make room for and to create greater inducements for white immigration that the South very much needs. Some thousands of negroes going north every year and a corresponding number of whites coming south would affect a distribution of the races that would be in many ways beneficial and that at the very least would take away from the race problem all sectional aspects, which is and has always been the chief cause of sectional ill feeling. And it would in the end give the South a homogeneous citizenship.

The *Vicksburg Herald* [2] was of the opinion that:

Adjustments and compensation will, we have faith, come. The northern drift as it continues, and carries thousands with it, will lower negro congestion in certain sections of the South. Such a change, restrained and graduated against violent progression, promises ultimate benefit. In the South, the effect of losing thousands of negroes from lands in southern Mississippi is already . . . producing a wholesome farm diversification and economic stimulation. Then, too, a more equitable distribution of the sons of Ham will teach the Caucasians of the northern States that wherever there is a negro infusion, there will be a race problem—a white man's burden—which they are destined to share.

[1] New Orleans *Times Picayune,* December 15, 1916.
[2] August 19, 1916.

Among those holding the view that the South needed the negro was the *Memphis Commercial Appeal*.[1] Concerning this an editorial in this paper said that not only does the South need the negro, but that he should be encouraged to stay.

The enormous demand for labor and the changing conditions brought about by the boll weevil in certain parts of the South have caused an exodus of negroes which may be serious. Great colonies of negroes have gone north to work in factories, in packing houses and on the railroads.

Some of our friends think that these negroes are being taken north for the purpose of voting them in November. Such is not the case. The restriction of immigration because of the European war and the tremendous manufacturing and industrial activity in the North have resulted in a scarcity of labor. The negro is a good track hand. He is also a good man around packing houses, and in certain elementary trades he is useful.

The South needs every able-bodied negro that is now south of the line, and every negro who remains south of the line will in the end do better than he will do in the North.

The negro has been a tremendous factor in the development of agriculture and all the commerce of the South. But in the meantime, if we are to keep him here, and if we are to have the best use of his business capacity, there is a certain duty that the white man himself must discharge in his relation to the negro.

The business of lynching negroes is bad, and we believe it is declining, but the worst thing is that the wrong negro is often lynched. The negro should be protected in all his legal rights. Furthermore, in some communities, some white people make money at the expense of the negro's lack of intelligence. Unfair dealing with the negro is not a custom in the South. It is not the rule, but here and there the taking of enormous profits from the labor of the negro is known to exist.

It should be so arranged that the negro in the city does not have to raise his children in the alleys and in the streets. Liquor in the cities has been a great curse to negroes. Millions of dollars have been made by no account white people selling no account liquor to negroes and thus making a whole lot of negroes no account. Happily this business is being extinguished.

The negroes who are in the South should be encouraged to remain there, and those white people who are in the boll weevil territory should make every sacrifice to keep their negro labor until there can be adjustments to the new and quickly prosperous conditions that will later exist.

Among those holding the same view that the South needed the negro was the *Georgia Enquirer Sun* of Columbus, Georgia.[2]

[1] October 5, 1916.
[2] December 2, 1916.

An editorial in this paper said that not only does the South need the negro but that he should be encouraged to stay.

The *Enquirer Sun* further emphasized the fact that the South needs the negro:

With the certainty that a number will differ with us, we state that the negro is an economic necessity to the South. Our plantations are large, our climate is peculiar, and we ourselves are not accustomed to doing the work that we ask the negro to do. Serious labor conditions have confronted us before, and it is exceedingly rare to find the native land owning white farmer, who has been accustomed to employ negro labor, taking the negro's place when the negro leaves his neighborhood. The same conditions exist in the industries where we of the South have been depending upon the negroes as artisans in our industries or mines.

The South has refused to accept immigration as a means of supplying our demands for labor. The farmers stand up and howl about preserving the pure blood of the South and invent all sorts of reasons for prohibiting the immigration of the same classes of people who have been making the North and East rich for years; the same classes that build the eighth wonder of the world—the Middle West. Now, if we are going to prohibit immigration, we must consider the economic status sufficiently seriously to preserve the only reliable supply of labor which we have ever known. That is the negro. We should ponder over the situation seriously and not put off until tomorrow its consideration, because this movement is growing every day. We should exercise our influence with our landlords and our merchants to see that a fairer division of profit is made with the negro and should watch the prices charged him as well as the interest charged him. We should see that the industries offer and pay to him a full and fair wage for his labor which will compare favorably with the wages offered in the East. We should see to it that the police in our towns, cities and counties cease making distinction between the negro and the white man when the negro is not absolutely known to be a criminal. When we do these things, we will keep our labor and we need to keep it.

In connection with the discussion of the need of the South for the negro, the duty of the South to the negro was pointed out. According to the *Columbia* (S. C.) *State*:[1]

If the southern white people would have the negroes remain, they must treat the negroes justly. If they refuse to do so their hope of keeping negro labor is in the unwillingness of the North to treat them justly, and we fear that this hope is more substantial than the North likes to admit. Justice ought to be cultivated everywhere for its own sake. Surely common sense will dictate to the South that it ought to forestall the

[1] December 22, 1916.

disruption of our industrial establishment by causing negroes to understand that they are safe where they are.

The Macon *Telegraph* said of negro labor: "If we lose it, we go bankrupt." Yet this same paper only a few months before was advocating the sending of 100,000 negroes into Mexico to conquer the "mongrel breed," and at the same time rid the South of that many worthless negroes.

The black man has no quarrel with the Mexican, but, on the other hand, he certainly has a disagreement with conditions as they affect him in the South, and, when he desires to improve those conditions by getting away from them, he must be checked. Plenty of "sound advice" is given him about staying in the South among his friends and under the same old conditions. The bugaboo of cold weather is put before him to frighten him, of race antagonism and sundry other things, but not one word about better treatment is suggested to lighten the burden, no sane and reasonable remedy offered.

The black labor is the best labor the South can get, no other would work long under the same conditions. It has been faithful and loyal, but that loyalty can be undermined, witness the exodus.

A letter published in the Montgomery *Advertiser* [1] truly says:

And the negro will not come back once he leaves the South.

The World War is bringing many changes and a chance for the negro to enter broader fields. With the "tempting bait" of higher wages, shorter hours, better schools and better treatment, all the preachments of the so-called race leaders will fall on deaf ears.

It is probable that the "well informed negro," who told the Birmingham editor that it was good schools that were drawing the negro, could have given other and more potent reasons had he been so minded. He could have told how deep down in the negro's heart he has no love for proscription, segregation, lynchings, the petty persecutions and cruelties against him, nor for the arresting of "fifty niggers for what three of 'em done," even if it takes all of this to uphold the scheme of civilization.

From Savannah alone, three thousand negroes went, from sixteen year old boys to men of sixty years. There must be something radically wrong when aged negroes are willing to make the change. There is greater unrest among negroes than those in high places are aware.

Let the *Advertiser* speak out in the same masterful way, with the same punch and pep for a square deal for the negro, that it does for democracy and the right for local self-government.

What was the attitude of the northern whites toward the migration? Although the North had been accustomed to the adding of a million foreigners annually to her population, these newcomers were white people and as such did not occasion the

---

[1] *The Advertiser,* Montgomery, Alabama, September 22, 1917.

comment or create just the problems which a large influx of negroes created.   The migration of the negro attracted a great deal of public attention.   A wide and extended discussion of the movement was carried on through the press.   The attitude which the white people assumed toward the migrants was expressed in this discussion.

The *New Republic* of New York City [1] pointed out that the movement gave the negro a chance and that he, the South and the nation, would in the end, all be gainers.

When Austria found the Serbian reply inadmissible, the American negro, who had never heard of Count Berchtold, and did not care whether Bosnia belonged to Austria or Siam, got his "chance." It was not the sort of chance that came to the makers of munitions—a chance to make millions. It was merely a widening of a very narrow foothold on life, a slightly better opportunity to make his way in the industrial world of America.

In the beginning such a migration of negroes would increase the present race friction in the North. Within certain limits a racial minority is unpopular directly in proportion to its numbers. Only as it increases to the point where political and economic power makes it formidable, does it overcome opposition. The negro's competition for jobs and homes will probably exacerbate relations. As the negroes increased in numbers they would not only seek menial and unskilled work, but also strive to enter skilled trades where they would meet with antagonism of white workers. Moreover, the negroes would be forced to seek homes in what are now regarded as "white" neighborhoods, and a clamor would be raised at each new extension of their dwelling area.

The antidote to persecution, however, is power, and if the northern negroes are more numerous and more urgently needed in our industrial life, they could protect themselves from the worst forms of discrimination. If by 1930 the negro population of the North has become three millions, instead of the fraction over one million which it is today, and if these three millions live better and save and spend more per capita than today, they will profit more than they will lose from their greater numbers. Their custom will be more valuable, their political power greater and, as wage earners, they will be strong enough to strike. Once they have completely filled a new neighborhood, opposition will cease. Moreover, the industrial competition with white workmen, while severe at certain crucial points, should not permanently be dangerous, since the very conditions which bring the negro north also make for higher wages for the white workers. What the white wage earner desires is not an industrial exploitation of the negro, but the maintenance of the white man's superiority of position.

For the nation as a whole, such a gradual dissemination of the negroes among all the States would ultimately be of real advantage. If at the end

[1] July 1, 1917.

of half a century, only 50 or 60 per cent, instead of 89 per cent of the negroes, were congregated in the southern States, it would end the fear of race domination, and take from the South many of its peculiar characteristics, which today hamper development. To the negro it would be of even more obvious benefit. The race would be far better educated, considerably richer, and with greater political power. Success for the negroes of the North would mean better conditions for southern negroes. For if the southern negro, finding political and social conditions intolerable, were able to emigrate to the North, he would have in his hand a weapon as effective as any he could find in the ballot box.

The Oshkosh, Wisconsin, *Daily Northwestern* felt that a large influx of colored people would bring to the North the same perplexing problems that long have disturbed the people of the southern States.

This, in fact, is the most serious aspect of this reported migration of southern blacks, and it is suggestive of no end of trouble for some of the northern States, which heretofore have regarded the so-called negro problem as something which little concerns them. The South has struggled for years to solve this problem, with its many phases and angles, and never yet has found a satisfactory solution. Should the same baffling questions be forced on the North it would give the people something to think about, and many will gain a new appreciation of the perplexities of the southern whites. And the necessity of facing this new problem may come to the North much sooner than generally is expected.

The Springfield, Massachusetts, *Union*[1] was also of the opinion that:

The North has been strong for the negro, considered as a political entity, but our communities are manifestly not desirous of supplying a field for him to expand and adapt himself to the social structure, and their leaders experience more difficulty in this regard than do their co-laborers in the South, with its vast colored population. This in itself furnished food for careful thought.

In a way, there is justification for a disinclination on the part of New Englanders to add a large negro element to their number. We have enough of a problem already to absorb and educate the large alien element that has come into our midst from the Old World. Our duty toward our colored residents should not go unrecognized, and the first step toward a just and fair disposal of related problems is to admit frankly that a rather strict color line is being drawn among us.

[1] July 16, 1916.

The Beloit, Wisconsin, *News* [1] held that the migration had brought the negro problem north and made it national:

The negro problem has moved north. Rather, the negro problem has spread from south to north; and beside it in the South is appearing a stranger to that clime—the labor problem.

It's a double development brought about by the war in Europe, and the nation has not yet realized its significance. Within a few years, experts predict the negro population of the North will be tripled. It's your problem, then, or it will be when the negro moves next door.

Italians and Greeks are giving way to the negroes in the section gangs along northern railroads, as you can see from the train windows, and as labor agents admit. Northern cities that ·had only small colored populations are finding their "white" sections invaded by negro families, strangers to the town. Many cities are in for the experience that has befallen all communities on the edge of the North and South—gradual encroachment of colored folks on territory occupied by whites; depreciation in realty values and lowering of rents, and finally, moving of the white families to other sections, leaving the districts in possession of colored families with a small sprinkling of whites.

This means racial resentment—for the white family that moves to escape negro proximity always carries, justly or not, a prejudice against the black race. It hits your pocket too.

Negroes will enter trades now monopolized by white men, at first, perhaps, as strike breakers; later, as non-union competitors, working for smaller wages. It will take some time, probably, to get them into the labor unions' way of thinking.

Politicians, both good and bad, will seek the ballot of a large new element, which will vote largely in the lump. Now, what will be the effect in the southern States? Already the offers of better jobs further north have caused strikes among southern negroes—something almost unheard of The South gets no immigration, but the negro has been an ever present source of cheap labor. With the black tide setting north, the southern negro, formerly a docile tool, is demanding better pay, better food and better treatment. And no longer can the South refuse to give it to him. For when the South refuses the negro moves away. It's a national problem now, instead of a sectional problem. And it has got to be solved.

The *New York Globe* [2] said that:

For more than a year a migration of men and women of color to northern States has been going on that has already deprived thousands of southern farmers of cheap labor. And the movement bids fair to continue. That it will have both good and bad effects is obvious. It will distribute the negro population more evenly throughout the States and thus tend to diminish race friction. But unless there is a change of spirit on

[1] August 25, 1916.
[2] July 31, 1916.

the part of northern unions, it will increase the danger of labor troubles in case of industrial depression.

The Pittsburgh *Dispatch*[1] held that the migration was helping the negro. It was of the opinion that:

This movement eastward and westward of unskilled negro labor will both directly and indirectly help the negro. The younger element, those of ambition and of some training in the schools, will be constantly emerging from unskilled to the semiskilled classes, with a consequent increase in their pay rolls and a betterment in their methods of living.

A decidedly better treatment of the negro, both in the North and the South, will grow out of the fact that the demand for his labor has been limited and the supply unlimited.

In the spring of 1918 the Walla Walla, Washington, *Bulletin*[2] summed up the situation thus:

There was much alarm a year or two ago over the migration of negroes to the North in large numbers. It was felt that they had far better stay in the South, in a familiar and congenial environment, and keep on raising cotton and food, than crowd into the inhospitable North for unaccustomed factory work. We have heard less of that lately; it is still doubtful whether the change is good for the negro himself, and there's no question that his coming has complicated housing conditions and social problems in northern cities. But economically the matter appears in a new light. At a time when war industries were starving for labor, the negro provided the labor. He is recognized as a new industrial asset.

The migration has been unfortunate, to be sure, for the communities thus deprived of agricultural labor; but it is said that from a broad, national standpoint the gain to the manufacturing industries more than compensates. And there has been an actual increase in the output of energy. The negro works harder in the North. He produces more. He is thus of more use to the community. And for the benefit he brings, communities are more willing than they were at first to tolerate the inconvenience due to his coming.

Some of the negro newspapers opposed the migration. Prominent among these was the *Journal and Guide* of Norfolk, Virginia, and the *Voice of the People* of Birmingham, Alabama. In speaking against the migration, the *Journal and Guide*[3] said:

[1] October 1, 1916.
[2] March 13, 1918.
[3] March 24, 1917.

It is difficult, if not impossible, to check the operation of an economic law, and it is perfectly natural that men should seek fields of labor in which they are promised higher wages and better conditions, but those who go and those who encourage the going of them should get the facts of the so-called inducements and learn the truth about them before lending their influence to a movement that can not only promise no permanent good to laborers, but works untold injury to the foundation of their own economic structure.

Another phase of the matter, and one that invites the condemnation of all honest persons, is the manner in which negro labor is at present exploited to satisfy the selfish whims of a group of misguided and ill-advised agitators and fanatics on the race question. All of the nice talk about "fleeing from southern oppression," and going where "equal rights and social privileges" await them is pure buncombe. It is strange that negro labor should stand the oppression of the South for fifty years and suddenly make up its mind to move northward as an evidence of its resentment.

The truth of the matter is that the element of negroes in the South that feel the oppression most is not concerned in the migration movement. Nor are they going to leave their homes and accumulations of half a century as a solution of their problems. They are going to remain here and fight out their constitutional rights accorded them here in the land of their birth.

The editor of *The Star of Zion,* Charlotte, North Carolina,[1] conceded the right of the negro to go wherever he had opportunity to go; on the other hand, it was doubtful whether a wholesale exodus was for the best. He said:

While I concede the black man's right to go where he likes, for he has the right of liberty and the pursuit of happiness, yet I doubt the wisdom of such wholesale exodus from the South. There are some things which the negro needs far more than his wages, or some of the rights for which he contends. He needs conservation of his moral life.

In the North a negro is brought face to face with new problems; among the many is the problem of adjusting himself to the abundance of freedom into which he comes so suddenly. His new freedom brings him new changes, as well as new opportunities, for among the roses there lies the thorn. . . . While the inducements of the North are very alluring, in the end the negro problem must be wrought out in the South.

Concerning the *Journal and Guide's* position, the Raleigh, North Carolina, *Independent* [2] took issue and said:

Our disagreement with our estimable contemporary, the Norfolk *Journal and Guide,* we are persuaded, is far less real than seeming. Essentially we

[1] July 19, 1917.
[2] April 28, 1917.

are in accord. We are certain that the *Journal and Guide* is not advocating the limitation of the negro to any one section of the country. If the exigencies of the present war have created a demand for his labor in the North at better wages than he can secure in the South like other people, he should take advantage of it and plant himself firmly in the industrial life of the section.

There are two ways by which we may improve our condition in this country. The one is segregation—voluntary segregation. The other is "scatteration." If we can come together, build up communities of our own, promote them into towns and even cities, we shall do well. If, on the other hand, we shall scatter all over the land and have nowhere a numerical congestion, we strengthen our cause.

The *Dallas* (Texas) *Express* [1] said:

The strangest thing, the real mystery about the exodus, is that in all the Southland there has not been a single meeting or promoter to start the migration. Just simultaneously all over the South about a year ago, the negro began to cross the Mason and Dixon line. Indeed, this is a most striking case where the negro has been doing a great deal more thinking than talking, knowing he is not given the freedom of speech. Who knows, then, what the providence of God is in this exodus. This exodus is not by any means confined to the worthless or the ignorant negro. A large per cent of the young negroes in this exodus are rather intelligent. Many of the business houses in Houston, Dallas and Galveston, where the exodus is greatest in Texas, have lost some of their best help. To tell the truth more fully, the negroes generally throughout the South are more dissatisfied with conditions than they have been for several years and there are just reasons why they should be. Every negro newspaper and publication in this broad land, including pamphlets and books, and the intelligent negro pastor with backbone and courage are constantly protesting against the injustices done the negro. And possibly these agents have been the greatest incentives to help create and crystallize this unrest and migration.

How the negro should be treated and what would hold him in the South was discussed at length and on many occasions in the columns of the *Atlanta* (Georgia) *Independent*.[2] An example of this discussion follows:

Last week we discussed at length the negro exodus. We tried to point out in plain, simple and manly language the reason and remedy for moving north. We warned our white neighbors that city ordinances and legislation could not stem the tide; that humane treatment would do more to settle the negro's industrial and economic unrest than anything else; that the

[1] August 11, 1917.
[2] January 27, 1917.

South was his natural home and he desired to stay here; but in order to keep him at home he must have contentment; he had to be assured of protection of life and property; assured of the enjoyment of public utilities; assured of educational advantages, ample and adequate, to prepare his children for useful and helpful citizenship; he must be permitted to serve God unmolested and to assemble in the community where he lives, in church, in society and politics; for his own moral, intellectual and physical benefit he must be given living wages and reminded in his daily dealings with his white neighbor that he is a citizen, not a negro, and that he is charged with responsibilities like other citizens. The negro is conscious of his racial identity and not ashamed of it. He is proud of his race and his color, but does not like to have the word "negro" define his relation as a citizen. The white man should understand that the negro is making progress; that he is getting property and education; that his wants are increasing in common with the white man's wants and that he is not going to be bottled up or hemmed up in any community, so long as there is another community on the face of the earth where he can breathe freely and enjoy the pursuits of life, liberty and happiness in common with other men.

The Christian Index [1] the official organ of the Colored Methodist Episcopal Church, published at Jackson, Tennessee, was of the opinion that:

There are two sets of causes for the negro leaving the South at this time. One set may be known as the surface causes and the other set beneath-the-surface causes. The surface causes are easily seen and understood These are economic causes. The war in Europe has called home foreigners out of the industrial centers of the North and West. These large factories and other industrial enterprises, representing enormous investments, had to turn in some other direction for labor. These large industrial opportunities with higher wages made strong appeals to the southern negro.

The beneath-the-surface causes are to be found in the handicaps under which the negro labors in the South and the uncivilized treatment to which he is subjected. He is segregated. To this he most strenuously objects. There is a difference between segregation and separation, especially so in the southern interpretation of segregation as observed in the practice of the South in its enforcement of the idea. Separation in matters social and religious is not necessarily objectionable. Left alone each race group instinctively seeks separation from other race groups. But segregation, as we have it, means more than separation; it means inferiority and humiliation. It means not only another section of the city for the negro, but a section that is inferior in improvement and protection; it means not only a different school, but an inferior school both in building and equipment; it means not only separate accommodations on the railroads, but

[1] June 24, 1917.

deplorably inferior accommodations; this, too, in the face of the fact that the negro pays the same price that is paid by others.

Another cause is the code of laws, or rather the practice of it, that gives more concern to the color of a man's skin than to the merits of a case he may have in the courts of justice. The negro is taught not to expect justice in the courts, however industrious, honest, law abiding he may be, when his lawful rights to liberty and protection are contested by a white man. The negro suffers in the courts, not always because he is guilty, not because he lacks character, but because his skin, not his heart, is black.

What was the attitude of the northern negroes toward the migration? With some exceptions, negroes north assumed a friendly attitude toward the migrants. Many of these residents of the North were themselves but recently come from the South. The newcomers were looked upon as brethren, just coming into the " Promised Land." They were welcomed in the churches and otherwise made to feel at home. In some cities there were organizations of resident negroes to look after the welfare of the new arrivals. In the northern race newspapers, the attitude of the negro north was fully set forth, as the following extracts from the *New York News* [1] indicate:

We hail with no alarm whatever the influx of colored men from the South. The colored people of the North will be strengthened by the hard working, ambitious laborers added to their numbers. The laboring conditions and life of the masses of the colored people in the South will be made better and brighter by their leaving.

Yet a heavy responsibility rests upon every colored leader, moral and civic, in these northern States to take an especial interest in their newly arriving brethren. You must teach them not to take their liberty to be ladies and gentlemen for license to degrade themselves and their race here. You must urge them to avoid the deadly vice and wasting extravagance of the unhealthy congested city. They should find their homes and rear their families in the suburbs, where they can buy their own homes and properly train their children in head, hand and heart. Urge them to get steady work and settle down. Urge them to become good citizens and better parents. Urge them to go to church, to lead patient Christian lives and all will come out well in the end.

The Philadelphia *Christian Recorder* [2] took the ground that:

1. The negro is an American. He speaks the language of the country and is, therefore, superior to the foreigner in this respect.

[1] September 17, 1916.
[2] February 1, 1917.

2. He knows the customs of the country and here again has the advantage of the foreigner.

3. He is a peaceable worker and is glad to have an opportunity to make good.

4. The negro is physically the equal and morally the superior of the immigrant from Europe.

There are reasons why the negro should succeed in the North. So we have no doubt that many will come.

Indeed, if a million negroes move north and west in the next twelve months, it will be one of the greatest things for the negro since the Emancipation Proclamation. And the movement of a million negroes should not alarm anybody, especially when we remember that a million immigrants were coming every year to this country before the war.

Let the good work go on. Let every community in the North organize to get jobs for our friends in the South. Let a million come. In coming the negroes will get higher wages.

They will get first class schools, running nine months a year—a thing worth leaving the South for, if there were no other advantages.

They will have a chance in the courts. If they should happen to have a difference with a white man, they will not take their lives in their own hands by standing up for their side.

They will be able to defend their homes, their wives and children in a way no negro can now protect them in the South.

They will have the right to vote. The foreigner must wait seven years for this—the negro only one year. If a million negroes come north, they will soon get sufficient political power, which combined with their economic power will be able to force the South to do some things she is now unwilling to do.

With labor competition for the negro between North and South with the North offering higher wages, better living conditions, better education, protection and a vote, the South must bestir herself if she would keep the best labor in the world. And southern statesmen will see that the South must cease to lynch, begin to educate and finally restore the ballot.

"But," says an objector, "these negroes coming north will increase prejudice." What if they do? Then the northern negro will sympathize more with his southern brother. But if prejudice increases, the negro has the ballot which is an effective way to combat it. If a million negroes come here we will have more negro businesses, better churches, more professional men and real political power, and the negro in the North will begin to get a social position not based on mere charity.

What were the causes of migration? A very large part of the discussion of the movement was taken up with setting forth the causes. The Montgomery *Advertiser* was of the opinion that the chief causes of the negro's leaving central Alabama were floods and the cotton boll weevil:

The negro from middle Alabama is going north because of economic conditions which he can not help and which he can not overcome. He is not being forced out by pressure from the white race. The relations between the two races in this section were never better; the negro is not subjected to oppression or or to any outbreaks of violence, which have induced the negro to leave certain sections of the South.

The negro is going because he is the most unfortunate of the victims of the combined disaster this year of the flood and the boll weevil. There have been actual want and hunger among some of the negroes on the planta- tions. The heads of negro families have been without present resources and without future prospects. The wise planter and farmer has said to his negro employes and tenants:

"You have not made anything this year. I have not made anything this year. But we will do our best and I will see what resources I can get together to keep you until next year, when we can all make a fresh start."

Another class of farmers, and we suspect that their number is too large, has said, "You never made anything this year. I never made anything this year. I can not afford to feed you and your family until the beginning of the next crop year. You must go out and shift for yourselves."

This cold blooded business view of the situation, we suspect, has been the best assistance that the labor agent has received. It is not difficult to know what a negro farm hand will do when he and his family are facing hunger, when a labor agent offers him a railroad ticket and a promise of two dollars and a half a day in the industrial works of the North and East.[1]

Lynching was one of the reasons most often given as a cause of the migration.

Current dispatches from Albany, Georgia, in the center of the section apparently most affected, and where efforts are being made to stop the exodus by spreading correct information among the negroes, say:

"The heaviest migration of negroes has been from those counties in which there have been the worst outbreaks against negroes. It is developed by investigation that where there have been lynchings, the negroes have been most eager to believe what the emigration agents have told them of plots for the removal or extermination of the race. Comparatively few negroes have left Dougherty county, which is considered significant in view of the fact that this is one of the counties in southwest Georgia in which a lynching has never occurred."

These statements are most significant. Mob law we have known in Georgia has furnished emigration agents with all the leverage they want; it is a foundation upon which it is easy to build with a well conducted lie or two, and they have not been slow to take advantage of it.

This loss of her best labor is another penalty Georgia is paying for her indifference and inactivity in suppressing mob law.

[1] *The Advertiser*, Montgomery, Alabama, December 12, 1916.

If Georgia is injured, agriculturally and industrially by the negro exodus, the white people here have no one to blame but themselves.

The indictment is true, every word of it. The appeal to humanity, to fairness and justice and right, has been apparently without effect. It is unfortunate for the people of Georgia that an appeal to the pocketbook should be necessary to bring back the enthronement of law, but if moral suasion is powerless, the question of personal interest has entered and in no uncertain degree.

The trouble incident to the migration of negroes from Georgia and the South is exactly as stated.

There is no secret about what must be done, if Georgia would save herself from threatened disaster, which, in some sections, has already become serious.

In the first place, there must be no more mobs. Mobs and mob spirit must be eliminated completely, so completely that there will be no danger of recurrence. If a negro be charged with a crime, even if it be known that he is guilty, he must be given the same fair treatment before the law that is accorded the white man. If anything, it would seem that ignorance and childishness demand even more consideration than the crime which lacks that excuse.

But more than that, we must be fair to the negro. There is no use in beating about the bush; we have not shown that fairness in the past, nor are we showing it today, either in justice before the law, in facilities accorded for education or in other directions. Argue it as you will, these things which we have not done are the things which we must do, or Georgia will suffer for it in proportion as she fails.[1]

In connection with lynchings there was the general fear of mob violence. This fear was taken advantage of by labor agents, as the following indicates:

We are astonished, too, to learn that one of the reasons for this unrest among the negroes who were born and reared here is fear that all negroes are to be run out of Georgia. This idea, of course, has been planted in the minds of the simple minded of the race by the crafty and unscrupulous labor agents who have operated in almost every section of the State.

The negroes have this idea from the fact that there are localities in the State right now where a negro can not live. And we do not know of anybody that is doing anything to change this condition.

Labor agents are doing their best to put the fear into the hearts of the negroes in this State that they are going to be run out by the white people, some of them even fixing the time as next June; but this work began long before the negro exodus north was thought of. The example of one county in north Georgia, which ran every negro out, was followed by other counties adjoining, and the general public has little idea

[1] *Atlanta Constitution,* December 10, 1916.

how widespread the contagion became—for lawlessness is nearly always contagious.

If Georgia is injured, agriculturally and industrially, by the negro exodus, the white people here have no one to blame but themselves. They have allowed negroes to be lynched, five at a time, on nothing stronger than suspicion; they have allowed whole sections to be depopulated of them; they have allowed them to be whitecapped and whipped, and their homes burned, with only the weakest and most spasmodic efforts to apprehend or punish those guilty—when any efforts were made at all.

Has not the negro been given the strongest proof that he has no assured right to live, to own property nor to expect justice in Georgia?

When the negro is gone, his loss will be felt in every large agricultural section and every industrial community of the South. For 'the average white man can not do the heavier work at the sawmills, naval stores plants and in many lines of manufacture, that is now being done by the negro. As a consequence, these plants and many large plantations must stand idle or import a class of white labor that will be a great deal worse than the black. Confronted with cheap white labor, and white men of a race of which they have no understanding—then will the South have its labor problems.

But at present, it seems, little can be done. Unless southern white people who have their all invested in agriculture or manufacturing take care of their own interest by seeing that the negro gets justice when suspected and a fair trial when accused, and assured that so long as he behaves he will be guaranteed safety of life and property, it is perhaps as well to let the negro go. It will mean an industrial revolution for the South, but the present condition of affairs has become intolerable.[1]

The negroes of the South used both the white and negro newspapers of that section in carrying on the discussion of the migration movement. The substance of what the negroes said through the press was that, first of all, the negroes wanted to stay in the South and were going north not only because there they could secure better wages than were generally paid in the South, but also because they would, in the North, get protection and have privileges not accorded in the South. Concerning the negro wanting to stay in the South, it was pointed out that in the South he did have economic opportunity and received encouragement. "The truth is that the negroes who are leaving the South in large numbers, and others who are thinking of going, do not want to go. They prefer to remain here." [2]

[1] *Georgia Gazette*, reprint from *Atlanta Constitution*, December 10, 1916.
[2] *Age Herald*, Birmingham, Alabama, September 25, 1916.

It was pointed out that the passing of stringent labor laws would not stop the exodus. The negro could not be kept in the South by force.

Various communities [said a negro] are passing stringent laws with the view of making the business of agents either impracticable or impossible. This will ultimately have the very opposite effect of what was intended. I am a negro and know the deeper thoughts and feelings of my own people. I know their yearnings and the religious zeal with which they look forward to the future for better days, and to other climes than this for better conditions.

Now to pass severe laws to block this movement will not only be a waste of time, but the most unwise way of dealing with the problem. The problem can not be solved from the angle of force.

In order for the negro to be kept in the South he must be made to see, to feel, that on the whole it will be better for him to remain in the South than to migrate to the North. Stop lynching. Teach us to love the South and be contented here by ceasing to abridge us in such extremes in common rights and citizenship.

Another method of helping to keep the negro in the South is for the better class of whites to get hold of the negroes. In a word, there should be cooperation between the races. The negroes should be given better schools and the whites should set before the negroes better examples of law and order. The North is offering better homes, better schools and justice before the law. The South can do the same.

"One of our grievances," said a negro correspondent of the *Chattanooga Times*,[1] "is that in colored localities we have very bad streets, no lights, no sewerage system, and sanitary conditions are necessarily bad. Give the negro the right kind of a show, living wages, consider him as a man, and he will be contented to remain here."

A good presentation of the negroes' side of the case is given in the following letter from a negro minister to the Montgomery *Advertiser*.[2] He wrote:

Why should the South raise such objections to the jobless man seeking the manless job, especially when it has held that jobless man up to the ridicule of the world as trifling, shiftless and such a burden to the South? Now the opportunity has come to the negro to relieve the South of some of its burden, and at the same time advance his own interests, a great hue and cry is started that it must not be allowed, and the usual and foolish method of repressive legislation is brought into play.

[1] Weldon Victor Jenkins, in *Chattanooga Times*, October 10, 1916.
[2] *The Advertiser*, Montgomery, Alabama, October 7, 1916.

Addressing the editor of the *Advertiser,* another negro correspondent said:

I have read with profound interest the many articles published in your paper upon the great negro exodus from the South.

The negro has remained in the South almost as a solid mass since his emancipation. This in itself shows that he loves the South, and if he is now migrating to the East, North and West by the hundreds and thousands, there must be a cause for it. We should do our best to find out these causes and at least suggest the remedy.

The time has come for plain speaking on the part of all. It will do us no good to try to hide the facts, because "truth crushed to earth will rise again." In the first place, the negro in this country is oppressed. This oppression is greatest where the negro population is greatest. The negro population happens to be greater in the South than in the North, therefore, he is more oppressed in the South than in the North.

Take the counties in our State. Some are known as white counties and others as black counties. In the white counties the negro is given better educational opportunities than in the black counties. I have in mind one Black Belt county where the white child is given $15 per year for his education and the negro child only 30 cents a year. See the late Booker T. Washington's article, "Is the Negro Having a Fair Chance?" Now these facts are generally known throughout this State by both white and black. And we all know that it is unjust. It is oppression.

This oppression shows itself in many ways. Take for example the railroads running through the rural sections of the South. There are many flag stations where hundreds of our people get off and on the train. The railroads have little stops at the platform about six feet square; only one coach stops at this point; the negro women, girls and boys are compelled to get off and on the train sometimes in water and in the ditches because there are no provisions made for them otherwise.

Again take the matter of the franchise. We all agree that ignorant negroes should not be intrusted with this power, but we all feel that where a negro has been smart and industrious in getting an education and property and pays his taxes, he should be represented. Taxation without representation is just as unjust today as it was in 1776. It is just as unfair for the negro as it is to the white man, and we all, both white and black, know this. We may shut our eyes to this great truth, as sometimes we do, but it is unjust just the same.

Take the matter of the courts. There is no justice unless the negro has a case against another negro. When he has a case against a white man, you can tell what the decision will be just as soon as you know the nature of the case, unless some strong white man will come to the negro's rescue. This, too, is generally known and the negro does not expect justice.

As yet, there has been no concerted action on the part of the white people to stop mob violence. I know a few plantations, however, where the owners will not allow their negroes to be arrested without the officer first consulting them, and these negroes idolize these white men as gods, and so far not one of these negroes has gone north. I repeat there are outcroppings of these oppressions everywhere in this country, but they show themselves most where the negroes are in the largest numbers. But all of this the negro is perfectly willing to endure, and they all may be classed as the secondary cause of this great exodus.

The primary cause is economic. The storms and floods of last July and August destroyed practically all crops in a large part of the South, and especially in the Black Belt section. These people are hungry, they are naked, they have no corn and had no cotton, so they are without food and clothes. What else can they do but go away in search of work? There are a great many wealthy white men here and there throughout the Black Belt section. They have large plantations which need the ditches cleared and new ones made to properly drain their farms. They could have given work to these destitute people; but what have they done? Nothing. They say that it is a pity for the negro to go away in such large numbers, and so it is, but that will not stop them. They have it in their power to stop them by making the negro's economic condition better here.

Thus far the average white man of the South has been interested in the negro from a selfish point of view; he must now become interested in him from a humanitarian point of view. He must be interested in his educational, moral and religious welfare. We know that we have many ignorant, vicious and criminal negroes which are a disgrace to any people, but they are ignorant because they have not had a chance. Why, I know one county in this State today with 10,000 negro children of school age, and only 4,000 of these are in school, according to the report of the Superintendent of Education. We can not expect ignorant people to act like intelligent ones, and no amount of abuse will make them better.

Sometimes we hear it said that the white man of the South knows the negro better than anybody else, but the average white man of the South only knows the ignorant, vicious and criminal negro better than anybody else. He knows little of the best class of negroes. I am glad to say, however, that there are a few southern white men who know the better class, and know them intimately, and are doing what they can to better the negro's condition. I would to God that the number of these few could be increased a hundredfold.[1]

R. R. Wright, President of the Georgia State Industrial College for Negroes, in a discussion of the causes of the migration movement stated that it is undoubtedly true that the high wages offered is the main cause. There are other aiding causes, however, for this movement besides low wages.

Naturally the negro is peculiarly adapted to a southern cli-

[1] W. J. Edwards, Principal of Snow Hill Normal and Industrial Institute (Colored), Snow Hill, Alabama, in the *Advertiser,* Montgomery, Alabama, January 27, 1917.

mate and prefers to remain in the South. He has made his best progress in the South. There are nearly a million negro farm operators and most of them are in the South. The total acreage of their farms is 42,279,510: valued at $1,141,792,526. In the value of farms operated there was an increase of 128.5 per cent, during the last census decade, while the value of farm property operated by white farmers for the same time increased only 99.6 per cent. The negro is prospering in the South. Now this and other facts constitute for the negro a strong tie to the southern soil.

This tie should not be broken lightly. The negro does not want to leave the South. The only thing to break this tie is unfair and cruel treatment of the negro on the part of the white man. In this connection our white friends should know that not only in the lynchings, and in the courts and in the unwholesome conditions on the southern railway common carriers (as vital as these are), but that in the general attitude of many of our southern white people, there is exhibited a contempt for the negro which makes the best of the negroes feel that they are only tolerated in the South. And yet in their individual relations there is no better friend to the negro in the world than the southern white man. In the face of our friends it is hard to explain this discounting and this contemptuous attitude, and yet everybody understands that it exists. "You are only a negro and are not entitled to the courteous treatment accorded to members of other races." Another cause is the feeling of insecurity. The lack of legal protection in the country is a constant nightmare to the colored people who are trying to accumulate a comfortable little home and farm.
There is scarcely a negro mother in the country. who does not live in dread and fear that her husband or son may come in unfriendly contact with some white person so as to bring the lynchers or the arresting officers to her door, which may result in the wiping out of her entire family. It must be acknowledged that this is a sad condition.
The southern white man ought to be willing to give the negro a man's chance without regard to his race or color; give him at least the same protection of law given to any one else. If he will not do this, the negro must seek those north or west who will give him better wages and better treatment.[1]

One of the most thoughtful discussions of the causes of migration was by W. T. Andrews, a negro lawyer and editor, formerly of Sumter, South Carolina. In an address before the 1917 South Carolina Race Conference he said:

[1] Reprinted from the *Morning News,* Savannah, Georgia, January 3, 1917.

In my view the chief causes of negro unrest and disturbance are as follows: the destruction of his political privileges and curtailment of his civil rights; no protection of life, liberty and property under the law; Jim Crow car; residential and labor segregation laws; no educational facilities worthy of the name in most of the southern States. These, I believe, are the most potent causes which are now impelling the southern negro to seek employment and find homes in northern and western sections of the country.

In South Carolina, and I believe it is equally true of every southern State, except those classed as "border States," statute after statute has been passed to curtail the rights of the negro, but in not a single instance can a law be pointed to which was enacted for the purpose of enlarging his opportunity, surrounding himself and his family with the protection of the law, or for the betterment of his condition. On the contrary every law passed relating to the negro has been passed with the intent of controlling his labor and drawing his circle of freedom into smaller and smaller compass.

In the rural districts the negro is not only at the mercy of the lawless white individual citizen, but equally at the mercy of the rural police, the constables and magistrates. There is hardly a record in modern history of greater oppression by judicial officers than that dealt to the negroes by a large majority of the magistrates and other officials who preside over the inferior courts of South Carolina.

In towns and cities, as a rule, mayors' and recorders' courts are mills for grinding out negro convicts; negroes charged with petty offenses are brought into these courts, convicted and sentenced with lightning speed, before they even realize that they are on trial unless they are able to hire attorneys, whose fees often equal the fine that would be imposed. They are beaten at will by arresting officers, frequently shot and many killed if attempt is made to escape by running away from the officer, and for any such shooting, officers are seldom put to the inconvenience of trial, even if the victim die.

In tragic truth it must be confessed that there is in the South—South Carolina, more certainly—no protection for the life or person of any negro of whatever standing, sex, age, against the intent of the bloody-minded white man.

The negro does not ask for special privileges or social legislation in his behalf. He does not ask to be measured by any standard less than the white man's standard, but he insists that the same test shall apply to all men of all races. He refuses to accept the declaration of men who claim to be earthly agents and representatives of the Almighty, the interpreters of His will and laws, and who solemnly assert that the God of the Christian ordained and decreed the negro race to be in slavery or semislavery to the white race.

The negro believes that the world is built on a moral foundation with justice as its basic rock. He believes that the Almighty is just, merciful and benevolent, and that He included all men in His plan of human development and reaching out for protection.

He asks only for justice. Nothing less than justice will stay the movement of negroes from the South. Its continued refusal will drive in the next two years a third or more of its negro population to other portions of the country.[1]

[1] From an address by W. T. Andrews at the South Carolina Race Conference, Columbia, South Carolina, February 8, 1917.

BIBLIOGRAPHY

Books and Periodicals

A Century of Negro Migration. C. G. Woodson, Washington, 1918.

The Negro Migrant in Pittsburgh. Abraham Epstein, Pittsburgh, 1918.

Negro Newcomers in Detroit. G. E. Haynes, New York, 1918.

The Migration of a Race, 1916-1917, Annual Report of National League on Urban Conditions among Negroes.

The 1917 Report of the Chicago Branch of the National League on Urban Conditions among Negroes.

Negro Migration: What Does It Mean? Gilbert N. Brink (pamphlet issued by American Baptist Home Mission Society, New York).

Negro Migration. *New Republic,* January 1, 1916.

How the War Brings Unprophesied Opportunities to the Negro Race. *Current Opinion,* December, 1916.

Negro Moving North. *Literary Digest,* October 7, 1916.

Cotton Pickers in Northern Cities. H. B. Pendleton, *Survey,* February 17, 1917.

Exodus in America. *Living Age,* October 6, 1917.

Lure of the North for Negroes. *Survey,* April 7, 1917.

Negroes Come North. K. Moses, *Forum,* August, 1917.

Negroes Go North. R. S. Baker, *World's Work,* July, 1917.

Negro Migration. P. H. Stone, *Outlook,* August 1, 1917.

Negro Migration as the South Sees It. *Survey,* August 11, 1917.

Passing of the Jim Crow. W. E. B. DuBois, *Independent,* July 14, 1917.

Reasons Why Negroes Go North. *Survey,* June 2, 1917.

South Calling Negroes Back. *Literary Digest,* June 23, 1917.

Southern Negroes Moving North. *World's Work,* June, 1917.

Welcoming Southern Negroes; East St. Louis and Detroit a Contrast. F. B. Washington, *Survey,* July 14, 1917.

When Labor Is Cheap. B. M. Edens, *Survey,* September 8, 1917.

Interstate Migration. W. O. Scroggs, *Journal Political Economy,* December, 1917.

Negroes Move North. G. E. Haynes, *Survey,* May 4, 1918.

Negroes a Source of Industrial Labor. D. T. Farnham, *Industrial Management,* August, 1918.

Negro Welfare Workers in Pittsburgh. *Survey,* August 3, 1918.

Negroes and Organized Labor. *Survey,* February 9, 1918.

Negro and the New Economic Conditions. R. R. Moton, Proceedings National Conference of Social Workers, 1917.

Migration of Negroes into Northern Cities. G. E. Haynes, National Conference of Social Workers, 1917.

Progress of Work for the Assimilation of Negro Immigrants in Northern Cities. F. B. Washington, National Conference of Social Workers, 1917

Negro Migration. Ralph W. Tyler, *Pearsons,* November, 1917.

Southern Labor as Affected by the War and Migration. Monroe N. Work, Proceedings of Southern Sociological Congress, 1918.

The Duty of Southern Labor during the War. R. R. Moton, Proceedings Southern Sociological Congress, 1918.

The Foundation (Atlanta), May-June, 1917.

A. M. E. Church Review (Philadelphia), January, 1917; April, 1918.
Voice of Missions (New York City), June, 1917.
Causes of Migration from the South. W. T. Andrews, Address at Race Conference, Columbia (S. C.), February 8, 1917. Specially printed.
The Massacre of East St. Louis. Martha Gruening and W. E. B. DuBois, *The Crisis*, September, 1917.
The Crisis, October, 1916, page 270; June, 1917, pages 63, 65.
The Nation, September 6; December 7, 1916.
The Problem of the Negro Laborer. *Iron Trade Review*, April 12, 1917.
Negro Migration Ebbs. *Iron Trade Review*, December 13, 1917.
Proceedings of Annual Convention of Federation of Labor, 1916, 1917, 1918.

Newspapers

(References for 1915, 1916, 1917, 1918)[1]

Akron (Ohio) Press, July 12, 1917.
Albany (N. Y.) Argus, Nov. 12, 1916.
Albany (N. Y.) Journal, August 6, 1917.
Albany (N. Y.) Knickerbocker Press, Dec. 21, 1916; Mar. 11, 26, 1917.
Amsterdam (New York City) News, May 28, June 18, 1915; Apr. 17, July 14, Aug. 18, Oct. 1, Dec. 13, 1916; Jan. 24, Aug. 1, 1917; Apr. 10, May 1, June 5, July 10, 24, Sept. 18, Oct. 2, 1918.
Artisan (Jacksonville, Fla.), Aug. 5, 1916.
Ashland (Ohio) Press, Aug. 22, 1917.
Asheville (N. C.) Citizen, July 11, 1917.
Atlanta Constitution, Aug. 23, 28, 1915; Sept. 13, 23, Oct. 10, 16, 18, 22, 24, Nov. 1, 4, 24, 26, 28, Dec. 1, 2, 4, 7, 8, 13, 21, 29, 1916; Jan. 8, 10, Mar. 10, 26, 31, May 14, 23, 26, 27, 29-31, June 5, 6, 11, 16, July 7, 13-15, Aug. 13, 30, Sept. 1, Oct. 24-26, Nov. 11, 21, 1917; Feb. 27, Mar. 2, Apr. 2, 4-6, 9, 17, 20, 24, 25, May 2, 7, 10, 21, 26, 27, June 2, 7, 8, 18, 22, 29, July 10, 15, 16, 18, 19, 25, 27, 28, Aug. 2-4, 10, 15, 19, 21, 25, 26, 30, Sept. 1, 21, 1918.
Atlanta (Ga.) Independent, Dec. 2, 9, 16, 23, 1916; Feb. 24, Mar. 31, May 9, 19, 26, June 30, July 21, 1917; Mar. 22, July 20, 27, Aug. 3, 17, 31, 1918.
Atlanta (Ga.) Journal, Oct. 8, 1917, Mar. 28, 1918.
Atlanta (Ga.) Post, June 26, Aug. 9, 1917.
Augusta (Ga.) Chronicle, Feb. 18, 19, Dec. 9, 1917; Mar. 29, 1918.
Aurora (Ill.) News, Feb. 7, 1918.
Baltimore Afro-American, Jan. 26, Sept. 29, 1917; Apr. 19, May 24, June 21, 1918.
Baltimore American, Nov. 17, 1916; Aug. 9, 1918.
Baltimore News, Aug. 13, 1915; Nov. 17, 1916; Apr. 3, 1918.
Baltimore Sun, Mar. 1, 1915; Sept. 21, Nov. 1, 20, 1916; Apr. 1, Aug. 13, 1917; Mar. 13, 1918.
Bath (Me.) Times, July 31, 1917.
Beaumont (Tex.) Enterprise, Sept. 2, 1917; June 20, 1918.
Beaumont (Tex.) Journal, June 24, 1917.
Beloit (Wis.) News, Aug. 25, 1916; Apr. 24, 1918.
Birmingham (Ala.) Age-Herald, Mar. 20, Sept. 25, Nov. 9, Dec. 2, 1916; Mar. 21, Apr. 2, Dec. 24, 1917.
Birmingham (Ala.) Ledger, May 3, 21, 24, 31, July 31, Sept. 27, 1917; Apr. 23, 1918.
Birmingham (Ala.) News, Aug. 31, 1917; June 21, 1918.

[1] The newspaper discussion of the migration had its beginning in 1915 in statements about the conditions of negro labor in the South and the outlook for it in the North. The discussion was continued in the 1918 newspapers.

Birmingham (Ala.) Reporter, July 28, 1917; Aug. 10, 17, Sept. 28, Oct. 5, 1918.

Boston Christian Science Monitor, May 24, 1916; Jan. 4, July 10, 27, Sept. 25, 1917; Jan. 28, 1918.

Boston Globe, Mar. 23, 1917; Mar. 30, 1918.

Boston Guardian, May 6, Aug. 22, 27, Oct. 10, 1916; Feb. 3, June 16, Aug. 4, 25, Oct. 6, 1917.

Boston Herald, Mar. 23, July 5, Sept. 13, 1917.

Boston Post, Feb. 26, 1917.

Boston Transcript, July 13, Dec. 15, 1916; Mar. 10, 31, Apr. 3, July 3, 7, 1917.

Bridgeport (Conn.) Farmer, Jan. 8, 1917.

Bridgeport (Conn.) Post, Oct. 7, Nov. 21, 1916; June 24, 1917; Jan. 24, 1918.

Bristol (Va.) Courier, July 29, 1917.

Bronx (N. Y.) Record and Times, Oct. 20, 1917.

Brooklyn Eagle, Aug. 10, 1917; Mar. 28, May 12, 21, July 25, Oct. 6, 1918.

Brunswick (Ga.) Banner, Oct. 10, 1917.

Buffalo (N. Y.) Courier, Sept. 16, 1917.

Buffalo (N. Y.) Express, Apr. 14, Oct. 23, Nov. 17, Dec. 7, 1916; June 15, 1917; Apr. 2, 1918.

Buffalo (N. Y.) News, Jan. 1, Aug. 31, 1917; June 18, 1918.

Buffalo (N. Y.) Times, Dec. 7, 1916; Nov. 20, 1917.

Burlington (Vt.) Free Press, Oct. 14, 1916.

Camden (N. J.) Courier, Apr. 30, 1918.

Charleston (S. C.) News and Courier, Oct. 26, Nov. 6, Dec. 18, 20, 1916; Jan. 2, Feb. 1, 23, Mar. 14, 1917.

Charlotte (N. C.) News, Mar. 11, 1918.

Charlotte (N. C.) Observer, July 17, Sept. 2, 1917; Mar. 28, Apr. 13, May 23, June 21, Sept. 21, 1918.

Chattanooga (Tenn.) Times, Dec. 15, 1916; Dec. 7, 1917.

Chester (S. C.) News, Aug. 13, 1918.

Chicago American, Nov. 20, 1916.

Chicago Defender, Mar. 16, 23, 30, Apr. 5, 27, 1915; every issue for 1916; every issue for 1917; almost every issue to Oct., 1918.

Chicago Examiner, Oct. 9, 1916; Mar. 30, July 19, 1917.

Chicago Herald, Oct. 13, 1916; Mar. 4, 19, July 3, 5, Oct. 10, Nov. 17, 1917.

Chicago Idea, June 30, 1917.

Chicago Journal, May 30, July 19, 1918.

Chicago News, Dec. 11, 13, 1916; Jan. 13, Mar. 20, 30, Apr. 21, July 31, Sept. 14, 1917; Jan. 15, Apr. 29, July 13, Aug. 7, 1918.

Chicago Tribune, July 25, 1916; June 9, July 8, 10, 26, Sept. 14, Oct. 27, 1917; February 13, 1918.

Christian Century (Chicago), July 25, 1918.

Christian Index (Jackson, Tenn.), June 21, July 19, Oct. 18, 1917; Feb. 21, Aug. 8, 1918.

Christian Recorder (Philadelphia), Aug. 3, 17, Sept. 14, Oct. 26, Nov. 9, 15, Dec. 21, 1916; Jan. 4, Feb. 1, Mar. 10, June 7 (special edition), Aug. 2, Sept. 20, 27, 1917; Jan. 24, Mar. 28, Apr. 11, 25, May 9, Aug. 1, 8, 15, 22, Sept. 19, 1918.

Cincinnati Commercial Tribune, Aug. 5, 10, Dec. 5, 1917; June 11, 1918.

Cincinnati Enquirer, Aug. 23, Oct. 30, 1916; Feb. 28, Mar. 26, Sept. 8, 12, 1917; July 31, 1918.

Cincinnati Post, Oct. 5, 1917.

Cincinnati Star, Sept. 12, 1917.

Cincinnati Union, Sept. 15, 1917.

Cleveland Advocate, Oct. 5, Sept. 14, 1915; Aug. 10, Nov. 11, 1917; Mar. 30, June 8, July 4, 27, Aug. 3, 10, 17, 1918.

Cleveland Leader, June 7, Dec. 8, 1916; July 10, 1917.

Cleveland News, Aug. 11, 1917.

Cleveland Plain Dealer, Oct. 19, 1916; Aug. 4, Sept. 12, Oct. 25, Dec. 6, 1917; Feb. 14, 1918.

Cleveland Press, Apr. 18, Oct. 25, 1917.
Columbia (S. C.) State, Oct. 2, 3, 7, 19, 23, Nov. 1, 15, Dec. 17, 22, 1916;
   Jan. 8, Feb. 2, Mar. 2, July 15, Oct. 20, Dec. 10, 1917; Mar 10, 1918.
Columbus (Ohio) Citizen, July 7, Aug. 7, Sept. 24, 1917.
Columbus (Ohio) Dispatch, July 8, Aug. 1, 20, Sept. 3, 20, 1917; May 8,
   June 30, 1918.
Columbus (Ga.) Enquirer-Sun, Nov. 21, Dec. 2, 17, 1916.
Columbus (Ohio) State Journal, Aug. 2, 21, 22, Oct. 10, Nov. 8, 1917;
   Aug. 6, 1918.
Cumberland (Md.) Times, July 7, 1917; Apr. 9, 1918.
Dallas (Tex.) Baptist Standard, Aug. 17, 1916.
Dallas (Tex.) Democrat, July 28, 1917.
Dallas (Tex.) Express, July 14, 21, Aug. 11, 25, 1917; July 20, 1918.
Dallas (Tex.) Journal, May 10, June 7, Sept. 24, 1918.
Dallas (Tex.) New Era, June 14, 1917.
Dallas (Tex.) News, Aug. 1, 1917; May 14, 16, 1918.
Dayton (Ohio) News, July 7, 30, Aug. 1, 1917; May 7, 1918.
Deep River (Conn.) Era, Nov. 9, 1918.
Denver (Col.) Star, July 28, 1917.
Detroit Free Press, June 18, Nov. 6, Oct. 23, 1916; Sept. 7, 1917; Mar. 23,
   Apr. 27, Sept. 28, 1918.
Detroit Journal, Nov. 15, 1916; June 20, Aug. 6, 1917.
Detroit News, Aug. 12, 1916; Oct. 21, 1917; Apr. 2, 7, May 19, 25, Sept. 13,
   16, 1918.
Detroit News Tribune, Aug. 12, Nov. 19, 1916.
Detroit Times, Apr. 12, 20, June 29, 1918.
Dublin (Ga.) Herald, July 26, 1917.
Duluth (Minn.) News Tribune, Oct. 9, Nov. 9, 1916.
Elizabeth City (N. C.) Independent, Nov. 30, 1917.
Elmira (N. Y.) Advertiser, Feb. 9, 1917.
Evansville (Ind.) Courier, June 21, 1917.
Fort Wayne (Ind.) Journal-Gazette, Oct. 22, 1916; Oct. 11, 1917; Aug. 22,
   1918.
Forth Worth (Tex.) Star-Telegram, Oct. 16, 1917.
Fort Worth (Tex.) Record, Oct. 6, 1916; Mar. 27, July 22, Nov. 3, 1917;
   May 4, Aug. 11, Sept. 22, 1918.
Galveston (Tex.) News, July 11, Aug. 3, 12, 17, 1917; Jan. 6, Sept. 20,
   1918.
Grand Rapids (Mich.) Press, Sept. 10, 1917.
Greenville (S. C.) News, Apr. 3, 1916; Mar. 29, June 18, Sept. 10, 1917.
Hackensack (N. J.) Record, Apr. 4, 1917.
Harrisburg (Pa.) Patriot, July 7, 1917.
Hartford (Conn.) Courant, Aug. 7, Dec. 18, 1916; Feb. 15, Sept. 19, 1917;
   Feb. 22, 25, Mar. 17, 1918.
Hartford (Conn.) Post, Mar. 17, Sept. 15, 18, Oct. 9, 15, 17, 18, 1917.
Hartford (Conn.) Times, Jan. 11, July 12, Oct. 9, 1917; Apr. 23, May 24,
   1918.
Henderson (Ky.) Gleaner, Aug. 24, 1916.
Hoboken (N. J.) Observer, Oct. 18, 1917.
Hotel Gazette (New York City), Oct. 20, 1917; July 13, 20, 1918.
Houston (Tex.) Chronicle, July 22, 1917.
Houston (Tex.) Observer, Oct. 21, 1916; July 7, Oct. 27, 1917; May 18,
   21, June 8, Aug. 3, 17, 1918.
Houston (Tex.) Post, files for 1916; files for 1917; June 20, July 29,
   Aug. 31, 1918.
Houston (Tex.) Press, Aug. 14, 1917.
Holyoke (Mass.) Transcript, July 10, 28, 1917.
Indianapolis Freeman, Nov. 26, Dec. 9, 1916; Jan. 6, 13, Mar. 31, June 2,
   Oct. 13, 27, 1917; Feb. 9, Mar. 2, May 25, June 6, 29, July 26, 1918.
Indianapolis Ledger, July 16, Sept. 9, 1916; June 9, 1917.

Indianapolis News, Nov. 9, 1915; Nov. 16, 22, 24, Dec. 8, 1916; Jan. 23, 1917; June 7, July 24, 31, 1918.
Indianapolis Star, Sept. 21, 1918.
Indianapolis World, Dec. 9, 1916.
Jacksonville (Fla.) Metropolis, Dec. 22, 1916.
Jacksonville (Fla.) Times Union, Aug. 14, Nov. 10, Dec. 22, 1916; Jan. 20, 1917; Apr. 4, 1918.
Jackson (Miss.) News, June 12, Nov. 11, 1917; May 7, 1918.
Jersey City (N. J.) Journal, June 30, Oct. 10, 18, 1917; July 19, 1918.
Johnstown (Pa.) Democrat, Nov. 2, 1916.
Kansas City (Kan.) Globe, Aug. 25, 1917.
Kansas City (Mo.) Star, Aug. 17, 1916; Mar. 11, 1917; Mar. 9, 1918.
Kansas City (Mo.) Sun, Aug. 11, Sept. 8, 1917.
Kansas City (Mo.) Times, Apr. 6, 1918.
Knoxville (Tenn.) Journal-Tribune, Aug. 3, Sept. 23, 1916.
Lancaster (Pa.) Labor Leader, Sept. 1, 1917.
Louisville Courier Journal, July 18, Dec. 5, 1916; Mar. 28, 1917; Aug. 4, 5, 7, 1918.
Louisville News, Sept. 9, 1916; Sept. 15, 22, 1917; Feb. 23, Mar. 9, June 1, July 6, 1918.
Louisville Times, Sept. 29, 1916; Aug. 6, 14, 16, Sept. 11, 1918.
Macon (Ga.) News, Feb. 14, Apr. 30, May 5, Aug. 27, Sept. 1, 29, 1918.
Macon (Ga.) Telegraph, Sept. 5, Oct. 10, 1916; Feb. 18, Mar. 18, June 14, Nov. 21, 1917; Jan. 28, Aug. 7, 17, Sept. 3, 22, 1918.
Manufacturers Record (Baltimore), June 29, 1916.
Marietta (Ohio) Leader, Aug. 7, 1917.
Mason City (Iowa) Globe-Gazette, Oct. 24, 1917.
Memphis Commercial Appeal, Aug. 20, Oct. 5, 24, 1916; Sept. 9, 1917; Jan. 5, Apr. 6, May 1, 9, 27, 1918.
Memphis Press, July 5, 1917; Apr. 4, Sept. 20, 1918.
Meridian (Miss.) Dispatch, June 25, 1918.
Meridian (Miss.) Star, Jan. 4, Aug. 7, 1917.
Michigan Tradesman (Grand Rapids), Dec. 12, 1917.
Milwaukee (Wis.) Journal, Jan. 11, 1917; May 30, 1918.
Milwaukee (Wis.) Leader, July 13, 1917; Mar. 29, 1918.
Milwaukee (Wis.) Sentinel, Sept. 22, 1916; July 27, Oct. 5, 1917.
Milwaukee (Wis.) Wisconsin, Oct. 3, 1916.
Minneapolis (Minn.) Journal, July 12, 1917; June 11, 12, 13, 14, 1918.
Mobile (Ala.) Register, Jan. 4, Aug. 19, 1917; Apr. 27, 1918.
Montgomery (Ala.) Advertiser, Jan. 5, 1915; Mar. 5, 17, Aug. 5, 9, 20, 23, 24, Sept. 10, 15, 17, 19-21, 24, 27, 29, Oct. 4, 16, 25, 29, Nov. 5, 7, 8, 22, Dec. 7, 9, 10, 12, 17, 19, 21, 27, 31, 1916; Jan. 6, 9, 13, 16, 23, 25, 27, Feb. 1, 7, 14, Mar. 2, Apr. 22, May 5, 12, 21, 24, 30, 31, June 1, 2, 6, 11, Sept. 26, Oct. 1, 1917; Jan. 20, Feb. 3, 8, 10, 18, Apr. 23-26, 29, May 2, 4, 6, 27, June 2, 3, 6, 18, 27, 29, July 5, 26, 31, Aug. 1-3, 10, 11, 23, 27, Sept. 4, 13, 1918.
Nashville (Tenn.) Banner, Aug. 31, Nov. 4, 14, 17, 1916; Mar. 1, 28, Oct. 7, Nov. 25, 1917; June 15, 1918.
Nashville (Tenn.) Globe, Apr. 20, 1917; Feb. 15, Mar. 29, 1918.
Nashville (Tenn.) Tennesseean, Aug. 27, Sept. 1, Oct. 2, 22, 1916.
National Enquirer, July 25, 1918.
Newark (N. J.) Ledger, Apr. 11, 18, 1918.
Newark (N. J.) News, Mar. 10, 17, 29, Sept. 24, 28, Oct. 2, 10, 30, 1917; Feb. 20, Mar. 26, Apr. 9, July 19, Sept. 28, 1918.
Newark (N. J.) Star, July 31, 1915; Nov. 20, 1916; Oct. 5, 9, Nov. 6, 9, 1917.
New Bedford (Mass.) Mercury, July 20, 1917.
New Bedford (Mass.) Standard, July 19, 1917.
New Britain (Conn.) Herald, Sept. 11, 1917.
New Haven (Conn.) Register, Sept. 11, 1917.
New Orleans Item, Sept. 8, 11, 1917; Feb. 10, Mar. 31, May 13, 15, 20, 1918.

New Orleans Times-Picayune, Oct. 1, 19, 26, Nov. 10, 28, Dec. 9, 12, 15, 18,
    1916; Jan. 1, 14, Mar. 9, 24, June 13, Sept. 4, 8, 15, 21, Oct. 5, 1917;
    Apr. 7, 30, May 12, 16, June 14, Sept. 21, 1918.
New Orleans States, July 24, Aug. 7, 28, Oct. 10, 1916; Nov. 3, 1917; Jan. 21,
    Apr. 6, July 23, 1918.
Newport (R. I.) News, Sept. 1, 1917.
New Philadelphia (Ohio) Times, Oct. 26, 1917; Mar. 17, 1918.
New York Age, Feb. 11, 18, Mar. 4, May 27, Aug. 19, 1915; May 24,
    July 20, 27, Aug. 24, 31, Sept. 14, Oct. 26, Nov. 15, 23, 30, Dec. 14, 21,
    1916; Jan. 4, 11, Feb. 1, 8, 15, 22, Mar. 1, 15, 22, Apr. 5, 19, May 3, 10, 24,
    June 7, 14, 21, July 5, 26, Aug. 21, Sept. 20, Oct. 10, 11, 18, Nov. 1, 8, 22, 29,
    Dec. 22, 1917; Jan. 26, 29, Feb. 9, 16, Mar. 2, 9, 23, 30, Apr. 6, 20, 21, 27,
    May 4, 11, 18, 25, June 2, 8, 20, 22, 29, July 6, 13, 15, Aug. 10, Sept. 14,
    21, 28, Oct. 5, 1918.
New York American, July 16, 17, Aug. 12, Sept. 20, 1917; June 23, 1918.
New York Call, Feb. 28, Sept. 15, 1915; Sept. 30, Oct. 10, Nov. 16, 29,
    Dec. 3, 1916; July 1, Aug. 8, 9, Sept. 28, Nov. 13, 22, 1917; Mar. 5,
    Apr. 26, May 30, June 8, 24, Aug. 26, 1918.
New York Commerce and Finance, Sept. 13, Nov. 8, 1916; Mar. 27, 1918.
New York Commercial, Oct. 24, 1916; July 14, 1917.
New York Globe, Feb. 10, 18, Mar. 12, 1915; July 31, Oct. 25, Nov. 13,
    Dec. 6, 1916; Mar. 19, Apr. 9, Aug. 20, Oct. 9, 1917; June 5, Oct. 1,
    1918.
New York Herald, June 10, 1917.
New York Journal, July 14, Aug. 25, 27, Oct. 12, 1916; Oct. 4, 11, 1917.
New York Journal of Commerce, Aug. 14, 1917.
New York Mail, Feb. 27, 1915; Nov. 1, 1916; Aug. 1, Sept. 20, 1917;
    Feb. 6, 12, Mar. 11, 15, 18, Apr. 30, July 1, May 3, 1918.
New York News, Mar. 4, 1915; Apr. 13, Sept. 11, 29, Dec. 21, 1916; Jan. 25,
    Oct. 10, 1917; Feb. 14, Mar. 23, Apr. 10, 11, 25, Aug. 22, 1918.
New York Post, Dec. 28, 1915; Oct. 5, Nov. 17, Dec. 1, 4, 16, 1916; Feb. 3,
    July 13, 14, 16, Sept. 19, 20, Oct. 15, 25, 29, 1917; Jan. 31, Feb. 15,
    June 22, Sept. 25, 1918.
New York Sun, Mar. 27, Nov. 19, 22, 1916; Jan. 15, 20, Mar. 21, Apr. 4,
    July 2, Aug. 7, 10, 15, Sept. 21, Oct. 5, Nov. 19, 21, 1917; Jan. 31,
    May 1, 17, June 19, July 1, 2, 7, Sept. 17, 22, 1918.
New York Telegram, Nov. 16, 1916; Sept. 9, 1918.
New York Times, June 11, Aug. 17, Sept. 10, Oct. 21, Nov. 5, 12, Dec. 17, 1916;
    Oct. 7, 1917; Jan. 21, Feb. 1, May 25, 1918.
New York Tribune, Oct. 22, Dec. 24, 1916; July 2, 21, 31, Oct. 16, 1917;
    Jan. 6, May 11, 22, Aug. 26, Sept. 22, 1918.
New York World, Oct. 29, Nov. 12, 19, 1916; Mar. 21, 1917; Feb. 14, 23,
    Apr. 14, 18, May 21, June 23, 25, 1918.
Norfolk (Va.) Journal and Guide, Sept. 9, Oct. 2, Nov. 18, 25, Dec. 2, 16,
    1916; Jan. 23, Feb. 2, 24, Mar. 3, 17, 24, Apr. 14, May 12, June 30,
    July 7, 25, 28, Sept. 11, 15, 22, 29, Oct. 6, 13, 20, Dec. 1, 1917; Feb. 2, 9, 16,
    Mar. 10, 23, 30, July 13, Aug. 10, 1918.
Norfolk (Va.) Virginian-Pilot, Oct. 20, 1916; Oct. 19, 1917; May 14, 1918.
Oakland (Cal.) Tribune, July 13, 1917.
Omaha (Neb.) Bee, Mar. 4, 1917; Mar. 24, 1918.
Omaha (Neb.) World-Herald, Feb. 3, 1917.
Oshkosh (Wis.) Daily Northwestern, July 28, 1916.
Palatka (Fla.) Advocate, Mar. 10, 1917.
Passaic (N. J.) Herald, Apr. 15, 1918.
Paterson (N. J.) Guardian, Sept. 22, 1917.
Peoria (Ill.) Journal, Nov. 23, 1917.
Philadelphia Bulletin, Mar. 12, June 29, July 26-28, 30, 31, 1917.
Philadelphia Inquirer, Feb. 24, Mar. 2, July 26-31, Dec. 14, 1917; Jan. 31, 1918.
Philadelphia North American, Aug. 9, 30, Nov. 24, 1916; Feb. 2, Mar. 27,
    July 26-31, 1917.

Philadelphia Public Ledger, May 11, 1916; Jan. 26, Apr. 6, July 16, 26-31.
 Aug. 26, 1917; Jan. 31, May 27, Aug. 2, 3, 14, 1918.
Philadelphia Record, Apr. 8, 1915; Dec. 9, 1916; Mar. 2, Apr. 1, July 26-31,
 1917; June 12, 1918.
Philadelphia Telegraph, Oct. 11, Nov. 21, 1916; July 17, 26-31, 1917.
Pittsburgh Chronicle, Oct. 17, Dec. 1, 1916.
Pittsburgh Courier, June 22, 1917.
Pittsburgh Dispatch, Oct. 1, Dec. 7, 1916; Feb. 26, Mar. 16, Dec. 17, 1917;
 Mar. 7, Apr. 11, 14, 1918.
Pittsburgh Gazette Times, Nov. 21, 1917; June 28, July 7, 1918.
Pittsburgh Leader, Nov. 1, Dec. 7, 1916; June 28, 1918.
Pittsburgh Press, Mar. 28, 29, 1917.
Pittsburgh Sun, Mar. 26, 1917; Apr. 11, 1918.
Portland (Me.) Express and Advertiser, Nov. 25, 1916.
Portland (Me.) Press, Aug. 10, 1917.
Portland (Ore.) Oregonian, Nov. 7, 1917.
Providence (R. I.) Bulletin, Nov. 11, 1916; Feb. 13, 1918.
Providence (R. I.) Journal, Aug. 17, 28, Oct. 29, Nov. 9, 20, Dec. 23, 1916;
 Aug. 7, 1918.
Providence (R. I.) Tribune, Dec. 22, 1917.
Raleigh (N. C.) Independent, Apr. 28, July 21, Sept. 15, Oct. 27, Dec. 22,
 1917; June 1, 29, 1918.
Raleigh (N. C.) News and Observer, Aug. 11, Oct. 4, Nov. 14, 1916.
Reading (Pa.) Telegram, Sept. 7, 1916; July 11, 1917.
Richmond (Va.) News Leader, July 6, 1917; June 4, 1918.
Richmond (Va.) Planet, Mar. 10, Apr. 7, 28, May 5, 19, June 23, Aug. 18,
 1917; Feb. 16, 28, Mar. 30, Apr. 20, June 8, July 6, 1918.
Richmond (Va.) Times-Dispatch, Aug. 26, 1916.
Rochester (N. Y.) Democrat Chronicle, June 5, 1916; Feb. 18, Mar. 27, 1917.
Rochester (N. Y.) Post Express, Nov. 11, 17, Dec. 8, 1916; Jan. 8, 1918.
Rochester (N. Y.) Times, Dec. 11, 1916.
Rochester (N. Y.) Union and Advertiser, Dec. 8, 1916.
Rome (N. Y.) Sentinel, Mar. 21, 1917.
Sacramento (Cal.) Union, June 16, 1917.
Saginaw (Mich.) Courier-Herald, Mar. 21, 1917.
St. Joseph (Mo.) News, Feb. 17, 1917.
St. Louis Argus, Aug. 25, Oct. 20, 1916; Jan. 6, Feb. 9, Mar. 23, June 1, 8,
 Sept. 14, Oct. 5, 1917; Mar. 15, 22, Aug. 9, Sept. 27, Oct. 4, 11, 1918.
St. Louis Globe-Democrat, Feb. 15, May 30, 31, July 2-18, 1917; March 28,
 1918.
St. Louis Post-Dispatch, Dec. 1, 10, 14, 1916; May 30, 31, July 2-18; Sept. 9,
 Nov. 3, 1917; May 10, 11, July 12, 18, Aug. 28, 1918.
St. Louis Star, May 30, 31, July 2-6, 8-13, 15-18, 1917.
St. Louis Times, May 30, 31, July 2-6, 8-13, 15-18, Aug. 11, 28, 1917.
Salina (Kas.) Union, Aug. 30, 1917.
Salt Lake City (Utah) Tribune, Mar. 4, 1917.
San Antonio (Tex.) Light, Sept. 10, 1916; May 14, Sept. 1, 1918.
San Jose (Cal.) Herald, Aug. 28, 1916.
Savannah (Ga.) Morning News, July 31, Aug. 2, 1916; Jan. 3, July 18, 1917;
 June 6, 1918.
Savannah Tribune, Aug. 5, 19, Sept. 9, 23, 30, Nov. 11, Oct. 28, 1916; Feb. 3,
 Mar. 31, Apr. 7, 28, May 10, 12, 17, 19, June 2, July 2, 1917; Feb. 13,
 Mar. 16, Apr. 13, May 20, July 20, 27, Aug. 3, 24, 1918.
St. Paul (Minn.) News, June 12, 14, 17, 1918.
St. Paul (Minn.) Pioneer Press, July 9, Oct. 5, 1915; Dec. 1, 1916; Aug. 6,
 1918.
Scranton (Pa.) News, Mar. 3, 1915.
Seattle (Wash.) Post, Dec. 15, 1916; Aug. 16, 1917.
Sharon (Pa.) Herald, Feb. 1, 1917.
Shreveport (La.) Times, July 18, Aug. 2, Oct. 6, 1917; May 28, 1918.

Southern Standard (Macon, Ga.), June 16, 1917; May 2, 13, 1918.
Southwestern Christian Advocate (New Orleans), Dec. 7, 1916; Jan. 4, 11, Mar. 1, 22, July 19, Oct. 18, 1917; Mar. 9, May 30, July 25, Aug. 22, 1918.
Spartanburg (S. C.) Journal, Sept. 11, 1917.
Spokane (Wash.) Chronicle, Dec. 11, 1916.
Springfield (Mass.) News, Mar. 6, 1918.
Springfield (Ohio) News, Aug. 2, 1917.
Springfield (Mass.) Republican, May 12, Sept. 8, 10, Nov. 1, 17, 27, Dec. 3, 1916; Jan. 17, 19, 21, 25, Feb. 15, Mar. 8-11, July 7, Aug. 8, Nov. 27, 1917; Jan. 20, May 15, 1918.
Springfield (Mo.) Republican, Sept. 9, 1917; Mar. 14, 1918.
Springfield (Mass.) Union, Apr. 16, 1915; July 16, Sept. 6, 1916; Apr. 2, 1917.
Star of Zion (Charlotte, N. C.), July 19, Aug. 16, 1917.
Steubenville (Ohio) Star, Aug. 4, 20, 1917.
Syracuse (N. Y.) Herald, July 17, 1917.
Syracuse (N. Y.) Journal, Aug. 4, 1917.
Syracuse (N. Y.) Post-Standard, Aug. 2, 1916; Oct. 10, 1917.
Tacoma (Wash.) News, May 25, 1918.
Tampa (Fla.) Times, June 8, 9, 1917.
Texas Freeman (Houston), Oct. 13, 1917.
The Daily Herald (Baltimore), Nov. 22, Dec. 17, 1917; Jan. 5, Feb. 16, Mar. 8, 16, 23, 27, 30, April 1, 2, 16, 17, 19, 22, May 11, 13, 17, 18, 28, 30, June 6, July 8, 31, Aug. 6, 1918.
The Economic World (New York City), Mar. 9, June 29, 1918.
The Living Church (Milwaukee), Dec. 22, 1917.
The Observer (New York City), Oct. 7, 1916.
The Piedmont (Greenville, S. C.), Mar. 16, 1917.
The Progressive Farmer (Raleigh, N. C.), Jan. 27, 1917.
The Public (New York City), Nov. 30, 1917; May 25, 1918.
The Standard (Chicago), July 16, 1917; Jan. 26, 1918.
The Voice of the People (Birmingham), Aug. 5, Dec. 2, 16, 1916; Apr. 22, May 19, July 14, 1917.
The Watchman (New York City), Mar. 1, 1917.
Topeka (Kas.) Plain Dealer, Dec. 20, 1916; June 29, 1917.
Toledo (Ohio) Blade, July 12, Aug. 20, 1917.
Toledo (Ohio) Times, June 14, 1917.
Trenton (N. J.) State Gazette, Aug. 10, Sept. 24, Oct. 8, Nov. 14, Dec. 3, 1917.
Trenton (N. J.) Times, July 28, Aug. 6, 1916; July 6, Sept. 18, 19, 21, 22, 28, Oct. 13, Dec. 3, 1917; Feb. 13, Mar. 9, Apr. 10, July 11, 1918.
Troy (N. Y.) Times, July 7, Nov. 1, 1916; Feb. 16, Mar. 28, July 25, 1917.
Utica (N. Y.) Observer, Nov. 17, 1916; Aug. 22, 1917.
Utica (N. Y.) Press, Sept. 15, 1917.
Valdosta (Ga.) Times, July 3, 1917; Jan. 29, 1918.
Vicksburg (Miss.) Herald, Aug. 19, 1916; July 7, Dec. 7, 1917; July 30, 1918.
Vicksburg (Miss.) Post, Nov. 9, 1917; July 31, 1918.
Walla Walla (Wash.) Bulletin, Mar. 13, 1918.
Washington (D. C.) Bee, Feb. 13, 1915; Nov. 11, 1917; Mar. 23, Aug. 17, 24, Sept. 7, 1918.
Washington (D. C.) Herald, Jan. 23, 1916.
Washington (D. C.) National Tribune, Nov. 10, 1916.
Washington (D. C.) Post, Dec. 4, 1916; Feb. 25, 1918.
Washington (D. C.) Star, Nov. 23, 1916; Apr. 2, July 18, 1917; Sept. 8, 1918.
Washington (D. C.) Times, Nov. 13, 1916; Sept. 8, 1918.
Waterbury (Conn.) Democrat, Feb. 8, Oct. 29, 1917.
Waterbury (Conn.) Republican, July 4, 1917.
Waterloo (Iowa) Courier, Apr. 3, 1918.
Watertown (N. Y.) Times, Nov. 17, 1916; Feb. 2, 1917.
Weekly Witness (New York City), Sept. 6, 1916.
Wesleyan Christian Advocate (Atlanta, Ga.), Mar. 22, 1917.

Westerly (R. I.) Sun, Nov. 8, 1916.

Wilmington (Del.) News, Dec. 1, 1916; Sept. 17, 1917.

Wisconsin Weekly Blade (Madison, Wis.), Jan. 18, Mar. 15, Apr. 5, 1917.

Women's Wear (New York City), July 12, 13, 21, Oct. 3, 1917; Jan. 23, Mar. 27, Aug. 5, 1918.

Yonkers (N. Y.) Herald, July 12, 1915.

Youngstown (Ohio) Telegram, Aug. 21, 1917.

Youngstown (Ohio) Vindicator, Jan. 9, Mar. 23, 1918.

INDEX

Adams, Henry, 4, 6.
Abbott, William, 84.
African Methodist Episcopal Church, 145.
Akron, migrations to, 57, 126.
Alabama: migrations from, 4, 7, 59, 63-74, 95-96, 107, 109; causes of migrations, 14-15, 20-21; Colonization Council, 5; efforts to check migrations, 72, 76; effects of migrations, 86.
Albany, migrations to, 56.
Albert Trostel Co., employment of negro labor, 114-115.
Allis Chalmers Co., employment of negro labor, 114.
Altoona, migrations to, 134.
Aluminum Ore Works, employment of negro labor, 100-101.
Amaca, Tom, 37.
American Baptist Home Mission Society, 144.
American Car & Foundry Co., employment of negro labor, 97.
American Cast Iron Pipe Co., employment of negro labor, 93.
American Federation of Labor, 147-148. See also Labor Unions.
American International Shipbuilding Co., employment of negro labor, 139.
American Steel & Wire Co., employment of negro labor, 108-109.
Andrews, W. T., 172.
Arkansas: migrations to, 3, 9, 65-68; efforts to check migrations, 72.
Armour & Co., employment of negro labor, 100.
Armstrong Association, 137-138.
Atlanta Constitution, 59.
Atlanta Independent, 162.
Atlanta Mutual Insurance Co., 64.

Badham, Henry L., 20.
Bailey, H. C., 128.
Banks, Edward T., 128.
Beloit: migrations to, 110-111; wages in, 111.
Beloit News, 159.
Bibliography, 175-183.
Birmingham *Voice of the People*, 160.
"Bloody Isle," The, 99.
Boll weevil, damage to cotton crops by, 14, 165.
Booker T. Washington Social Settlement, 114.
Bricklayers, wages of, 16, 86.
Brickmasons, wages of, 86.
Brink, Gilbert N., 144.
Brown Farm, 37.
Bryant, Lewis T., 141.
Buffalo, migrations to, 56, 67.
Building trades, negroes employed in, 122.
Bus boys, wages of, 17.
Butler, J. H., 75.
Butchers, wages of, 114.

Cantonments, construction of, in South, 84.
Capital, influence on migration of Northern, 47.
Carpenters: in Pittsburgh, 122; wages of, 16, 86.
Carter, R. A., 146.

Causes of migrations: Of 1879, 3-6; unemployment, 14-15, 59; failure of crops, 14-15, 165; wages, 14-16, 83; demand for labor in North, 14, 17-18, 28-29, 102, 111; lack of educational facilities, 18-19, 81, 83; treatment in courts, 19-20, 22, 83-85; fee system and street tax, 20-21; traveling accommodations, 21-22; lynchings and mob violence, 18-19, 22, 79-81, 83, 166-167; prejudice, 24-25, 83; between cities in North, 117; as expressed through the press, 152-174.
Champion Chemical Co., 128.
Charlotte *Star of Zion*, 161.
Chart showing extent and trend of migrations, 71.
Chattanooga Times, 169.
Chauffeurs, wages of, 114.
Chicago: migrations to, 45, 58, 66-67, 69, 102; opportunities, 29, 102; increases in negro population, 7, 51; housing, 102-106; wages, 17, 102-103, 114; welfare work, 103. *See also* East Chicago; Illinois.
Chicago Defender, 29-33.
Chicago Renting Agents Association, 103.
Chicago Women's Club, 103.
Chisholm, J. N., 37.
Christian Index, 163.
Churches: effects of migrations on, 86, 144; aid rendered by, 132, 144-147.
Cigar factories, employment of women in, 129.
Cincinnati, migrations to, 57, 125.
Cleveland, migrations to, 57, 126-127.
Cleveland Association of Colored Men, 128.
Cleveland Welfare Federation, 126.
Colonization Council, 4-5.
Colored Methodist Episcopal Church, 146.
Colored Protective Association, 137.
Columbia (S. C.) *State*, 155.
Columbus, migrations to, 7, 57, 126.
Commerce and Labor, Secretary of, 99.
Conferences to check migrations, 79-81, 83; in Ohio, 128; in New Jersey, 140; American Federation of Labor, 147-148; National League on Urban Conditions among Negroes, 143-144, 149.
Connecticut: demand for labor, 54; migrations to, 56, 58, 141-142; wages, 142. *See also* Hartford.
Connors, William R., 127.
Convict system, 3-4.
Cooks, 122.
Core makers, 129.
Correspondence, influence of, on migrations, 34, 69.
Cotton crop, failures of, 14.
Council of National Defense, 129.
Courts, treatment in: cause of migrations, 19-20, 22, 83-85; effects of migrations, 89.
Crawford, Anthony, 47.
Credit system, 92-93.
Crop failures, 14-15.
Cudahy Soap Factory, 109.
Culver, Charles M., 130.

185

A LONG WAY FROM HOME
by Claude McKay

'NEW WORLD A-COMING'
by Roi Ottley

RECOLLECTIONS OF SEVENTY YEARS
by Daniel A. Payne

LETTERS FROM PORT ROYAL
edited by Elizabeth Ware Pearson

NEGRO PROTEST PAMPHLETS
edited by Dorothy Porter

MODERN NEGRO ART
by James A. Porter

NEGRO MIGRATION DURING THE WAR
by Emmett J. Scott

THE AFTERMATH OF SLAVERY
by William A. Sinclair

THE KEY TO UNCLE TOM'S CABIN
by Harriet Beecher Stowe

WALKER'S APPEAL
by David Walker &
AN ADDRESS TO THE SLAVES OF
THE UNITED STATES OF AMERICA
by Henry Highland Garnet

THE NEGRO PROBLEM
by Booker T. Washington, et. al.

THE GARIES AND THEIR FRIENDS
by Frank J. Webb

AMERICAN SLAVERY AS IT IS
by Theodore Dwight Weld

ON LYNCHINGS
by Ida Wells-Barnett

ROPE AND FAGGOT
by Walter White